QK
192
G8
1973

Gunther
    Ethnobotany of western Washingto   P9-DXH-664
knowledge and use of indigenous plants by
Native Americans

Ethnobotany of Western Washington

Mrs. Ada Markishtum, a Makah of Neah Bay, Washington, weaving at a window in her home.

Ethnobotany of Western Washington

The Knowledge and Use of Indigenous Plants
by Native Americans

Revised Edition

By Erna Gunther

With illustrations by Jeanne R. Janish

University of Washington Press

Seattle and London

Ethnobotany of Western Washington was first
published in 1945 as Volume X, Number 1, of
University of Washington Publications in Anthropology.
Second printing, 1955
Third printing, 1958
Fourth printing, 1961
Fifth printing, 1964
Sixth printing, 1970
Revised edition, 1973
Second printing (paper), 1974
Library of Congress Catalog Card Number 45-4872
ISBN (cloth) 0-295-95268-7
ISBN (paper) 0-295-95258-X
Printed in the United States of America

All rights reserved. No part of this publication
may be reproduced or transmitted in any form by
any means, electronic or mechanical, including
photocopy, recording, or any information storage
or retrieval system, without permission in writing
from the publisher.

Frontispiece photograph by James O. Sneddon

QK
192
G-8
1973

PREFACE

In a general ethnography the uses of plants are usually treated in a very cursory fashion. This is probably due to lack of time on the part of the ethnographer as well as inability to be in the area at all seasons of the year. It was therefore deemed feasible to undertake a separate paper on ethnobotany covering an area which had cultural cohesion and sufficient environmental variability to give interest to the study.

Many colleagues have been most helpful in compiling this study. Until he left the University in the spring of 1937, Dr. George Neville Jones identified all the specimens brought from the field. Helping then, and even more since Dr. Jones has left, has been Mrs. Martha Reekie Flahaut, assistant in biology at the Washington State Museum, without whose infinite patience, wide knowledge, and kind cooperation many activities at the Museum would not be possible. The field work on the Quinault, Chehalis, Cowlitz, and Swinomish was partly done by Mr. Roger Ernesti, University fellow in anthropology. Mr. Foster Palmer and Miss Wilma Basford, both students in the College of Pharmacy, checked all the plants used medicinally with the standard works on pharmacognosy.

A key set of the specimens used is at the Washington State Museum. In addition to the standard herbarium specimens, an attempt was made to get a specimen of that part of the plant used at the season of the year when it was regarded as ready for picking. It is realized that both this collection and this study are far from complete, and possibly in some years a supplementary paper may be prepared.

ERNA GUNTHER

University of Washington
September 9, 1940

77-03473

PREFACE TO THE REVISED EDITION

In the period that has elapsed since the first publication of *Ethnobotany of Western Washington,* interest in the natural environment has increased, together with a desire to know how it was used by former local cultures. Ethnologists have long been aware of the rich knowledge of the environment by the local Indian cultures, and in some parts of the country such material has been published—often, however, hidden in the midst of long ethnographic details. Now a new audience has become interested in the environment and its uses not only by present society but also by those of the past. In studying the Indian uses of plants and knowledge of where they grew, one also realizes the changes that have taken place in the country with the passage of time and the introduction of an industrial society.

For updated and corrected information on the Quileute entries, the reader is asked to refer to Appendix I. This material was graciously provided by J. V. Powell of the Department of Anthropology and Sociology, University of British Columbia, who worked with the Quileute in 1970. For permission to reprint the article written by Powell in collaboration with Fred Woodruff, a member of the Quileute tribe at La Push and former chief of the Quileute Tribal Council, I am indebted to the authors and to the Sacramento Anthropological Society. I also wish to thank Jeanne R. Janish and C. Leo Hitchcock for permission to reproduce the superb drawings originally published in *Vascular Plants of the Pacific Northwest* (University of Washington Press, 1955-1969).

ERNA GUNTHER

March 1973
Seattle, Washington

CONTENTS

MAP

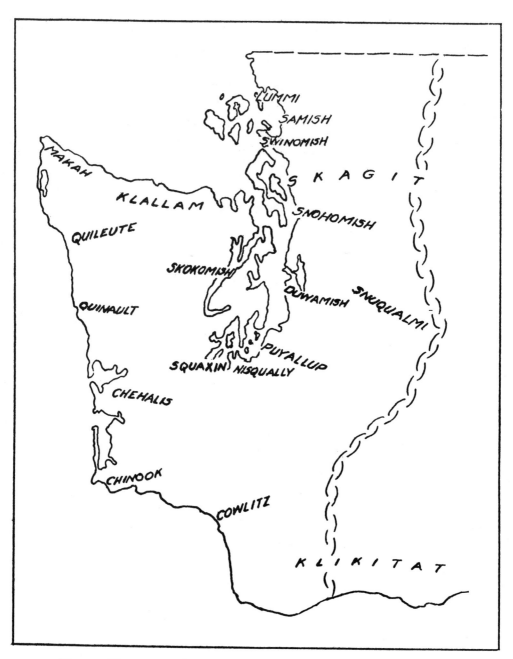

WESTERN WASHINGTON, SHOWING THE LOCATION OF THE VARIOUS INDIAN TRIBES

INTRODUCTION

Sporadically in ethnological literature there has appeared an ethnobotany, as that on the Tewa, the Zuni, the Thompson, to mention only a few published by the Bureau of American Ethnology. Two of these were written by anthropologists and the Thompson work was done by a botanist with anthropological training from an ethnologist's field notes. The phases of ethnography which demand scientific knowledge in another field are always difficult to approach because, to the specialists in each field, the work of the stranger in that field is found wanting. For compiling this material a knowledge of the floral environment with a good memory for taxonomy, but without the scientific basis for it, has been all the equipment this anthropologist could provide. Perhaps I could add to this catalog of qualifications a knowledge of the local cultures acquired through writing several ethnographies. In starting out, the bright hope of discussing the relationship between a people and their floral environment led me on, but I soon realized that the environment had changed too much, and the processes of acculturation had gone too far to achieve any such desirable results. Fifteen years ago I talked with old men who knew that bows were made of yew wood but had never used one seriously. A few had made them of commercial lumber as tourist souvenirs. Many an old woman wished she could dig camas for a meal but instead she cooks navy beans or macaroni. People of middle age have heard their grandparents talk of cedar-bark clothing and occasionally some culturally alert woman shreds some to make a dance costume (which, incidentally, she wears over her calico dress, and which is twined with raffia), but the cast-off clothing which white people trade for baskets, or clothing ordered from Sears-Roebuck has been the standard wearing apparel for them all their lives. On the other hand, sometimes features of the old culture—like medicinal usages—cling with amazing tenacity.

There is no need to reiterate the pressing necessity of ethnographic work in general, but it should be pointed out that ethnobotany is one of the fields of inquiry that must be done with even greater haste than some of the more subjective phases of the work. The area under consideration here has changed greatly in the past few generations, through deforestation and the introduction of weeds by farming. George Neville Jones in his introduction to *A Botanical Survey of the Olympic Peninsula*[1] makes this statement: "Two major catastrophic events have occurred in the recent history of the vegetation of the lowland areas of the Olympic Peninsula—the Ice Age and the Caucasian invasion." This is true not only of the Olympic Peninsula but of the entire area under discussion. So instead of working only against the dying out of people who participated in some of the old culture, here even the very materials on which the culture depended are disappearing and changing. The great cedar trees which yielded roots appropriate for basketry are harder to find, and small medicinal plants are no longer available within a short walk, because the wooded areas which supported them have been cut down and are at best a tangle of fireweed and blackberries.

TERRITORY

Since the state of Washington consists of two distinct climatic areas, the semi-arid region east of the Cascade mountains, and the forested country to the west, the territory set apart in this study is indicated by the physiography as well as by the Indian cultures. The westernmost portion borders on the Pacific Ocean and is designated largely as the Olympic Peninsula, still a very primitive area with unexplored regions in its highest mountains. This great mountainous area drops off to the south into the broad alluvial valley of the Chehalis River and to the east is bordered by Hood Canal and Puget Sound, both bodies of salt water. In this area are located the following tribes: at the most northwesterly corner, the Makah; 40 miles south on the Pacific coast, the Quileute at the mouth of the Quillayute River; further south, the Hoh, a division of the Quileute, at the mouth of the Hoh River; next the Queets, a division of the Quinault, who occupied the watershed of the Queets River just as the Quinault proper lived along their stream as far into the mountains as Lake Quinault and the upper river. It should be noted that these are the first people to penetrate the mountains to any extent. All the tribes mentioned went hunting in the Olympic mountains, but only the Quinault maintained villages as far from salt water as the upper Quinault River. It is also noteworthy that, with the exception of the Makah, each group centered around a river. On account of the denseness of the forests along the coast as elsewhere in this entire region, water transportation was the only feasible way to travel. What trails there were in the mountains were used only by hunters. The dependence on canoe travel put great stress on the building of seaworthy craft; and of all the wood work done by these tribes, the finest products were their canoes, sturdy yet graceful—some adapted for the fast water of the rivers, and others more commodious,

[1] Jones, George Neville, *A Botanical Survey of the Olympic Peninsula*, University of Washington Publications in Biology, 5, 1936.

for family travel. With the Quinault territory one reaches the southern boundary of the mountains, and the valley of the Chehalis, ending in Grays Harbor, presents a river people in an open country where oaks grow and grassy meadows, locally known as "prairies," are found.

One should not leave the Olympic Peninsula without mentioning the excellent description of the area in the introduction of Jones's *Botanical Survey of the Olympic Peninsula*, a book which has been one of the mainstays of this study.

Again on the salt water are the Lower Chinook, who lived on both sides of the mouth of the Columbia and north on the coast of Washington to Willapa Harbor. Leaving the ocean altogether, the Upper Cowlitz or Taitnepam inhabit the area known as the Big Bottom country toward the southwest slopes of Mount Rainier. This country is typical of the slopes of the Cascade mountains, in which range Mount Rainier is situated. Swinging around the shoulder of Mount Rainier the real "prairie" country is occupied by the Nisqually, and at the very head of Puget Sound by a salt-water people, the Squaxin, on Squaxin Island. In a landscape dominated once again by a river were the Puyallup, a group definitely divided, like so many Puget Sound people, into upriver and salt-water units. Just south of Seattle in the wide river valleys were several groups, today concentrated on the Muckleshoot Reservation. Typical of them is the Green River group. Then to the north of the modern urban area along the Snohomish River with its many sloughs, on the salt-water beaches of the mainland around Everett and on the southern end of Whidbey Island, were the Snohomish, with the Snuqualmi, an upriver people, in the same general latitude. Again a salt-water people, the Swinomish, who lived on Fidalgo Island, are contrasted with the Upper Skagit, who lived as far into the Cascades as any of the local tribes. They were at the western end of several important trails going to Lake Chelan and Lake Wenatchee in eastern Washington. Finally at the northern boundary of the area are two tribes, the Lummi on Lummi Island, with landscape very similar to the Swinomish, and the Klallam on the northern border of the Olympic Peninsula, where slightly more of the ocean-beach character exists.

Both the Olympic Peninsula and the region of western Washington between Hood Canal and the Cascades are well described by Dr. Jones in his introduction to the Olympic flora mentioned above and in his more recent publication, *The Flowering Plants and Ferns of Mount Rainier*.[2] He discusses the general aspects of the floral life as well as the climate and geology. It would be difficult to try to improve on the concise manner in which he has brought together his material. As a guide to the botany, only the Olympic flora paper was used, and

whatever changes have been made in his later publication have not been incorporated.

CULTURES

While this area has the linguistic diversity characteristic of the Pacific coast, it was chosen for its relative cultural homogeneity. The situation resolves itself into this: in an area where the flora is fairly uniform, there are many small tribes with cultures that are materially very much alike. Does this seeming homogeneity actually hold true in a careful examination of one phase of their material existence? How much diversity is there in their use of their floral surroundings? The specific tribes chosen were selected because of the environment in which they lived and because they exemplified certain local variations in this general culture pattern. They also represent five linguistic stocks. In describing the territory in the foregoing paragraphs each one of the groups was mentioned in its relation to its geographical environment. Their cultural relationships are also important to review.

Beginning again at the northwestern corner of the area, the Makah are the only Nootkan-speaking tribe within the United States. They share with their relatives on Vancouver Island the knowledge of the open ocean, and they are accustomed to go many miles off shore for whaling and sealing. They lived in a number of villages both on the Strait side and the ocean side of Cape Flattery. On the ocean beaches they found various grasses and seaweeds used by them alone, whereas the flora of the Lake Ozette region and the foothills is similar to that shared by other groups to the south. The Quileute have two rivers, the Quillayute and the Hoh, in their territory and depend more on salmon in the traditional western Washington style than the Makah, who go to the Swiftsure Banks for halibut. The Quileute and Hoh speak Quileute, a dialect of the Chemakuan stock. The Quinault furnished the Makah dried elk meat in return for whale oil and dentalium, an indication of their greater use of the mountain region of their territory. While the men went hunting alone, often the women went part way to a base camp and there became acquainted with the upland flora. It is a matter of chance perhaps, although I am not so sure, that the largest number of plants secured from any one group came from the Quinault. The tribe is represented in this study by Olson's excellent ethnography[3] as well as by field work.

From here there is a sharp slope in the cultural plane which has been gradually going downhill from Cape Flattery, but whose real peak is in the Queen Charlotte Islands. The Chehalis have no outstanding cultural attributes and were included here because of their locale in the Chehalis valley. Incidentally, they and the Quinault speak dialects of Coast Salish. To

[2] Jones, George Neville, *The Flowering Plants and Ferns of Mount Rainier*, University of Washington Publications in Biology, 7, 1938.

[3] Olson, Ronald L. *The Quinault Indians*, University of Washington Publications in Anthropology, 6, 1936.

the south are the Lower Chinook, historically as well as culturally a very important group. These people were extensive travelers and traders. This is the only group where the work included in this study is based entirely on the literature. Just recently a splendid study of the Lower Chinook was made by Dr. Ray,[4] a remarkable feat, since the group was regarded as practically extinct when Boas worked with Charlie Cultus in 1890. Dr. Ray's material was secured chiefly from one woman, Emma Luscier, at best a difficult informant. Several attempts made to do further work with her were unsuccessful. A little Chinook information was given by Miss Louise Colbert.

The Upper Cowlitz are again an upriver, mountain people who are of peculiar interest because they speak a Sahaptin dialect. A check of the Salish words for western Washington flowers as compared to the flora occurring on both slopes of the Cascades yielded so low a correlation that it seemed of no significance. Sahaptin and Salish words are used indiscriminately. The Nisqually and Puyallup represent southern Puget Sound cultures, speaking very closely related dialects of Coast Salish.[5] The "prairie" aspect of Nisqually makes the culture of special interest. More or less similar to the Puyallup is the Green River group, as indicated above, a modern combination of former small groups, never very clearly defined because of tribal exogamy, with little linguistic distinction and great overlapping of culture. The information on this area was largely secured through Mr. Arthur Ballard of Auburn, a careful student of the southern Puget Sound Salish.[6] The Snohomish represent a more homogeneous group living in a similar environment, more extensive in area and having better internal cohesion as a tribe; they are a river people with, however, an outlet to the salt water. Their "hinterland" neighbors are the Snuqualmi, a river group with access to the foothills where one would expect much the same results as those obtained from the Puyallup. Moving farther north, but still along rivers that run down from the Cascades, one finds the Upper Skagit. They speak a Salish dialect and have not been as directly influenced by the eastern Washington people as the Cowlitz, though geographically they were in a similar position for it. The difference between the Upper Skagit and the Lower Skagit around the mouth of the river and on Whidbey Island is largely a linguistic one. It was disappointing not to find greater contrasts. Whether there ever were any such contrasts that have now faded out of the culture cannot be determined with the information available, since no ethnographies have been done in either group.

This survey leaves only three northern groups which are a linguistic unit within the Coast Salish languages, the Swinomish on Fidalgo Island, the Klallam on the southern shore of the Strait of Juan de Fuca, and the Lummi on Lummi Island, at Marietta, and in the surrounding area. The Swinomish and Lummi share the general Puget Sound flora, whereas the Klallam, being well along on the Strait, have a little more of the beach flora also found in the Makah territory. A beginning toward the ethnobotany was incorporated in the author's study of the Klallam.[7] This information has been greatly augmented by more recent field work. A study of the Lummi by Stern[8] contains the mention of many plants but with no positive botanical identification. More field work was also done here. No ethnography of the Swinomish has been done, but the ethnobotany shows that in material culture at least there would be no striking innovations. It should be added that a meager account of the Snohomish and Snuqualmi, with scattered noted on the Nisqually, may be found in *The Indians of Puget Sound*.[9]

METHOD OF PROCEDURE

In order to achieve the greatest accuracy in identification of the plants, both by the Indian and in the herbarium, the same specimen was always the center of the discussion. Preferably these plants were picked on a walk with the informant. But since so many informants are very old, often bedridden, it was generally necessary to bring the plants to them. I tried as far as possible to bring them freshly picked plants, for they are not accustomed to the dried specimen, as is the botanist. Departure from this was sometimes necessary when it was too difficult to get the plants where the informant was living. Where possible, both a man and a woman from the same culture were used; women knew the food and medicinal plants and were more likely to give information on charms and potions; men knew the materials in nets, fishing gear, and wood working. This is understandable in the light of the division of labor. An effort was also made to visit the same group at various seasons but my academic schedule did not always permit this.

In summing up this procedure I am aware that in most cases I have only a list of plants known or used, while it had been my ambition to get some estimate of the botanical knowledge of the groups visited. Perhaps that goal was too ambitious; perhaps I did not allow enough time. I feel some explanation is due. Constant work with these people brings out

[4] Ray, Verne F. *Lower Chinook Ethnographic Notes*, University of Washington Publications in Anthropology, 7, 1938.

[5] Since this was written *The Puyallup-Nisqually* by Marian W. Smith (Columbia University Contributions to Anthropology, 32, 1940) has appeared. Some effort was made to incorporate the information into this study but it was too late to use it as effectively as might be desired.

[6] Ballard, Arthur C. *Some Tales of the Southern Puget Sound Salish*, University of Washington Publications in Anthropology, 2, 1927; *Mythology of Southern Puget Sound*, University of Washington Publications in Anthropology, 3, 1929.

[7] Gunther, Erna, *Klallam Ethnography*, University of Washington Publications in Anthropology, 1, 1927.

[8] Stern, Bernhard. *The Lummi*, Columbia University Contributions to Anthropology, 17, 1934.

[9] Haeberlin, H. and Gunther, E. *The Indians of Puget Sound*, University of Washington Publications in Anthropology, 4, 1930.

again and again the dearth of knowledge of many phases of the older culture. Some cultural habits adapt themselves to change, but where, as I explained before, the very forests have disappeared, the occasion for naming plants and using them is rare and consequently forgotten. It frequently happened that an informant said, "Where did you find this plant? I haven't seen it in years," or "I know that plant, but I can't call it"—meaning that he had forgotten the name. In a few instances when I happened to have a plant with me which I knew did not grow in the locality, I showed it to the informant as a kind of test. It was seldom turned away without a question as to where it came from, with a clear indication of awareness of its intrusive character. It was also valuable to get their reactions to adventitious plants. There was no agreement among informants, and I have no accurate way of judging their knowledge. Introduced plants did not reach all places in this area simultaneously. Also when the informant says it has always been here he may speak only from personal experience, and many introduced plants have been in the area through the life span of a fifty-year-old. However, the burdock, the Canadian thistle, and the daisy are all recognized as recently introduced. Some informants, like my Quinault woman, insisted on a trip to Spruce Orchard for plants we had not found near Taholah and was very accurate in leading me to small patches of certain plants. Knowledge of exact seasonal variation is also very good, especially as to the ripening of berries. Often only one name is used for several varieties of the same plant. Within a small area near a Klallam village I happened to pick three varieties of gooseberry. They had a separate name for *Ribes divaricatum* with its large thorns, but *R. lacustre* and *R. Lobbii* were regarded as the same. They recognize the difference between the willows but have only one name for them. But we must remember that in our culture only the rare person or the trained botanist has more extensive knowledge.

It must also be understood that the information secured in many cases was the knowledge of an individual who might be either more or less familiar with plants than the average person in the community. Generally, lack of interest also meant lack of knowledge and vice versa. In these cultures where medicinal knowledge was a matter of private property, there might be wide differences in information. The record here is a random sample.

The chart on pages 53-55 shows the range of plants used by each group and also reflects the uniformity of their presence. The absence of any plant is not evidence of its disuse. Wherever knowledge of a plant was denied after an informant had seen the specimen, note was made of the fact, because it was realized that mere absence of the plant in a list could not stand as negative evidence.

INFORMANTS

The general introduction to this study would not be complete without a brief discussion of the inform-ants without whose knowledge it could not exist. Their tribal background is important and in this region very unpredictable. The tribal groups are small and exogamy is very widespread. In the old pattern, patrilocal residence was the complement of exogamy and to a certain degree that allowed one to make reasonable inferences as to the group to which an individual belonged. But now, on account of reservation life many people are living away from their place of origin. Many also have spent years away at school so that even middle-aged persons have very little knowledge of old customs.

Listed according to tribes, the following were the principal informants used:

Chehalis. Mrs. Maggie Pete, between 60 and 70 years old, was born at Gate City of a Chehalis father and a Chinook mother. She has always lived on the Chehalis reservation and speaks her father's language. She was very cooperative, and had worked with anthropologists before. She was bedridden and could only discuss those plants brought to her.

Dan Susina or Secena, a man of about 80, whose father was Chehalis and mother half Skokomish and half Satsop. He lives near Mrs. Pete at Oakville. He worked with Miss Thelma Adamson on myths and texts.

Ed Smith, a brother of Mrs. Pete, now lives on Schneiders Prairie near Olympia but was born at Copalis of an Upper Chehalis father, and a mother half Chinook and half Lower Chehalis. It was possible to work with these Chehalis informants without interpreters and alone, which usually leads to better results. Mrs. Pete's daughter was frequently present but was a helpful rather than a disturbing influence.

Cowlitz. John Ike is an Upper Cowlitz living near Ethel. He was born at Mossy Rock, an old Cowlitz village site. Work with him usually resolved itself into a family conference, because he lacked confidence in his knowledge.

Mary Kiona is a delightful old woman of about 70, referred to by her uncle, Jim Yoke, from his heights of about 95 years as "that young lady." These two live together and both speak poor English but there was no interpreter available except a giggling grand-niece in her teens. It was more satisfactory to work without her. They live near Randle and had spent their lives in the Big Bottom country, knowing its outlet toward eastern Washington and the slopes of Mount Rainier rather than toward the Lower Cowlitz country. They are both Upper Cowlitz with some Yakima admixture.

Green River. This material was all secured from Mr. Ballard, an excellent local field worker who has lived all his life in Auburn and has known the surrounding Indians thoroughly since childhood. He also has a real working knowledge of the local languages.

Klallam. With the brief notes in my *Klallam Ethnography* as a beginning I returned for further work only to find all my old informants dead, with the exception of Robert Collier of Jamestown. In addition I found Mrs. Sam Ulmer, a Lower Elwah Klallam, who, with her husband, supplied much of the new information on this tribe. That she is hesitant about some older customs became clear when she prefaced the use of a love charm by this statement: "I'm a Christian now and don't do such things any more."

Lower Chinook. The bulk of the information was taken from Ray's *Lower Chinook Ethnographic Notes* with a few additions from Miss Louise Colbert, who is about one-eighth Chinook and a descendant of an historically important family.

Lummi. The Lummi material was first taken from Stern and supplemented by field work with Mrs. Annie Paul Cush Pierre, a Lummi living near Marietta. Her information was checked and added to at the house of Mrs. Lucy Celestin where she, her sister, and her sister's husband, all Lummi, went into long discussions among themselves over the plants presented. I am certain that many medicinal uses were not mentioned because of modesty in the presence of a man (the husband) and a stranger. The women mentioned them to each other in Lummi.

Makah. This whole study began through my work with Mrs. Ada Markishtum, one of the finest informants I have ever had. Both she and her husband are real naturalists with an intelligent and observant interest in their surroundings. Although Ada is half white, she was brought up by her grandmother as an Indian, so that she is more conversant with the old culture than her age would indicate. The only other Makah informant was her husband.

Nisqually and *Puyallup.* The occasional notes incorporated from Dr. Smith's study and a few words of Puyallup obtained from Mr. Ballard are the only sources for these tribes.

Quileute. The first Quileute material was secured by Mr. Roger Ernesti from Morton Penn, and I later added to it with Nina Bright and her sister Mrs. Leaven P. Coe. My visit was at a more advanced season and brought out much additional information. All these people are Quileute-Hoh mixtures, which keeps them well within one cultural group.

Quinault. The greatest array of informants was used in this tribe. Some were the same people who worked with Olson more than ten years ago. Billy Garfield and Alice Jackson are among the best informed members of the tribe, but age has dimmed their memories. Mrs. Julia Cole, a younger woman than Mrs. Jackson, was very practical and helpful, being the only one who actually went on collecting trips. Mr. Ernesti did the work with Billy Garfield and Mrs. Jackson.

Samish. The stray bits of Samish came through the presence in the home of Charles Edwards, when Mr. Ernesti worked there, of Mrs. Joshua, a half Samish, half Skagit. The tribal differences between Samish and Lower Skagit are very slight.

Skagit. It appears that the Upper and Lower Skagit have considerable differences in their culture, though perhaps not so great as the Upper and Lower Cowlitz, although I doubt that, in the case of the Upper Skagit, I secured information accurate enough to justify any real claims. Intermarriage and long visits have blotted out, in the remaining culture, all the finer distinctions. The working conditions in this group were difficult. Everywhere there was a mixed group who regarded my visit as a kind of radio quiz program, and consequently carefully considered information was not forthcoming. There was no way to break up these groups, nor could I get anyone to go on a collecting trip because of the constant rain. Mrs. Agnes Williams is part Skagit, part Samish, and probably gave me more Lower than Upper Skagit. Mrs. Annie Jones, whose daughter, Mrs. Martin, was a very unwilling interpreter, is Upper Skagit except for a Snuqualmi maternal grandfather. Mrs. Mary Washington is a pure Skagit but lived away from her tribe for a long time while she was married to a white man. Mrs. Mary Napoleon, the best of these informants, was also married to a white man for 20 years. Her memory for the uses of plants was good, but she did not know their names. Her cousin, Mrs. Harry Moses, would probably have been the best informant to use, but I found her last and since she was just about to leave for the remainder of the summer she was not in the mood for work.

Skokomish. The information on this tribe was secured in one visit to Mrs. Mary Adams, who turned out to be a more reliable informant than I anticipated.

Snohomish. The meager notes of Haeberlin and Gunther are filled out by work with Mrs. Elizabeth Shelton of Tulalip who remembers all the very obvious plants but has no real working knowledge of the less known ones. No other Snohomish informant seems to be available.

Snuqualmi. Another people like the Snohomish who have lived on a logged-off reservation too long to retain much of the older knowledge of plants, the Snuqualmi do not furnish any rich material today. Susie Williams worked with Mr. Ernesti.

Squaxin. This is another group which was included by chance because an informant was available. In working with Ed Smith on Chehalis, his wife, who is half Squaxin and half Chehalis, offered the Squaxin names and uses for plants discussed by her husband.

Swinomish. Tommy Bob, his wife, and Charles Edwards worked with Mr. Ernesti on winter botany which I supplemented in early summer with Mrs. Peter John and old Mrs. Samson. All these people are predominantly Skagit in their derivation but have spent most of their lives on Fidalgo Island.

ARRANGEMENT OF MATERIAL

With the mechanics aside, our attention should be focused on the kind of material secured and its arrangement in this monograph.

Since plants are the basis of this discussion the material has been put in botanical order, starting with the ferns. A miscellaneous group, poorly identified and incomplete, and the seaweeds, mosses, lichen and fungi appear at the end. The index is prepared in such a manner that plants can be located through their best known colloquial names.

Within each plant species, the information is arranged according to use, as food, materials, or medicine. The lists of native names at the head of each species show lucidly some of the linguistic borrowings which have taken place. The phonetic transcription is not uniform because it was done by too many people, but all variations are based on the *Phonetic Transcription of Indian Languages*, Smithsonian Miscellaneous Collections 66, 1916, No. 6.

THE PLANTS AND THEIR USES

POLYPODIACEAE
Fern Family

Fern leaves are widely used by all the local tribes in household work, lining and covering storage baskets of food, wiping fish, covering food in cooking vessels. Many ferns are also used medicinally, but only *Polypodium vulgare* (licorice fern) appears in any of the pharmacy references consulted.

The Quileute have a general name for ferns, pla'pla, and the Nisqually call them tɑ'di, but no indication was found of other family classifications.

Polypodium vulgare L. (*P. vulgare* var. *occidentale* Hook.; *P. falcatum* Kellogg; *P. Glycyrrhiza* D. C. Eaton; *P. vulgare* var. *commune* Milde; *P. occidentale* (Hook.) Maxon.) Licorice Fern.

Cowlitz	k'ɬwe·'ɬk
Green River	skiwĕlkᵘ[10]
Klallam	kla'sĭp[11]
Lummi	k'ᴇsī'p
Makah	xĕxi't, "crawling root on trees"
Quinault	tsumana'amats[12]
Skagit	kɬĕ'tcai
Snohomish	k!ĕtcai
Swinomish	stsɬoqwi'lkᵘ

Medicine. Wherever this plant is used in western Washington, it is for the medicinal purpose which is also cited in the materia medica.[13] The rhizome is roasted by the Makah, peeled, chewed, and the juice swallowed for coughs. The Cowlitz crush the rhizome, mix it with young fir needles, boil it, and drink the infusion for measles. The Quinault, who know the fact that it grows best on alder moss, either bake the root on coals or use it raw as a cough medicine.[14] Eells mentions the same for the Klallam[15] and Mr. Ballard for the Green River.

Reagan reports that this plant, as *P. occidentale* (Hook.) Maxon, is common at Grays Harbor, Lapush, Quillayute, Forks, East Clallam, and Neah Bay, and that it is chewed much by the Indians.[16]

Polystichum munitum (Kaulf.) Presl. Sword Fern.

Chehalis	sa'xalum
Cowlitz	tsɬi'mai[17]
Green River	sxa xltc

[10] Ballard.
[11] Eells, pp. 618, 623.
[12] Olson, p. 181.
[13] Stuhr, No. 630, *Glycyrrhiza glabra* L. roots used as a demulcent and laxative. U.S. Dispensatory: used as an expectorant in chronic catarrh and asthma, also a purgative; p. 1528. Youngken: *P. Lepidota* Nutt. used as expectorant, demulcent; p. 390.
[14] Olson, p. 181.
[15] Eells, pp. 618, 623.
[16] Reagan, p. 56.
[17] Joe Young through Ballard.

Klallam	pilapilaxiltc
Lummi	s'xĕ'lem
Makah	plĭpla'bupt; totoqwa's, "roots above the ground"
Quileute	pila'pila'bupt;[18] ts'ikwi', roots; tsato'tsa, young growth; pla'pla, all ferns
Quinault	sk'ĕ'ĕ'tckɬ; sk'okots'a, rhizome
Skagit	stca'lasets, whole plant; squĭ''ux, roots; saq!, roots
Snohomish	xa'xaltc
Squaxin	sxa'xaltc
Swinomish	sxa'xalɑtc; k'alanditc, small sprout

Food. The rhizome is peeled and baked in a pit and eaten by the Quileute with fresh or dried salmon eggs. The Quinault bake the rhizome in a pit on hot rocks, cover it with sword-fern leaves and sand, and build a hot fire on top. The same part is boiled and eaten by the Makah and Klallam.

Materials. The leaves of the sword fern are frequently used to line baking pits. The Quileute, Quinault, Chehalis, and Cowlitz use them in baking camas, the Cowlitz for wapatoo, and the Makah for steaming sprouts, while the Quinault use them for baking its own rhizome. The Squaxin spread the leaves on drying racks because berries do not stick to them. The leaves are used by the Quileute for mattresses. The Cowlitz tie the sword-fern leaves together with maple bark for the same purpose. The children of the Klallam and Makah play an endurance game, seeing who can pull off the largest number of fern leaves, saying "pila" with each one, on a single breath.

Medicine. The young, curled leaves are regarded as medicinally useful by the Swinomish, who chew them raw and swallow them for sore throat or tonsilitis; while the Quileute put the chewed leaves on salmonberry bark to cure sores and boils. The Green River tribe, according to Mr. Ballard, use the rhizome as medicine, and, more specifically, the Cowlitz wash sores with an infusion of the boiled rhizome. The Quinault boil the roots and wash hair in this water to cure dandruff. The spore sacs are scraped off the leaves by the Quinault and put on burns. The Lummi women chew the curled leaves to facilitate childbirth.

No reference is made to sword fern in any of the pharmacognosies consulted.

[18] Since the "bupt" suffix denotes "plant" in Makah, the Quileute may have borrowed this word.

Dryopteris dilatata (Hoffm.) Gray. (*Dryopteris spinulosa dilatata* (Hoffm.) Underw.; *Thelypteris dilatata* (Hoffm.) House.) Wood Fern.

Cowlitz	ts'kwai
Green River	tsō′kwĭ[19]
Klallam	tsa′qwa
Snohomish	k!lɑlk!ala′ts

Food. The Cowlitz bake the rhizomes overnight in a pit and then eat the inside. The Puget Sound tribes generally are credited with using these rhizomes for food, gathering them in the fall and winter during the dormant season of the plant.[20]

Medicine. The Klallam pound the roots and put the pulp on cuts. The Snohomish soak the leaves for a hair wash.

Athyrium Filix-femina (L.) Roth. (*A. cyclosorum* Rupr.; *A. Filix-femina* (L.) Roth, var. *sitchense* Rupr.) Lady Fern.

Cowlitz	qa′lqali
Quileute	tseqwĕ′ɛ′put, whole plant; tseqwĕ′, root
Quinault	kuwá·lsa; tsamxaih[21]

Food. On the Olympic Peninsula this fern as well as several others serves as food. Both the Quileute and Quinault eat the center of the rhizomes after they have been roasted and peeled. The Makah ate the "bulbs" on the root, and stated that the Klallam ate the new shoots.[22] The Quileute specify that the roots are baked in a pit overnight. The inside of the rhizomes is yellow. The Quinault dig these ferns in August and serve them mixed with dried salmon eggs.[23]

Materials. The Cowlitz use the leaves to cover camas while baking and the Quileute use them to wipe fish.

Medicine. The rhizomes are boiled by the Cowlitz and the tea drunk to ease body pains. The Makah pounded the stems of four ferns, boiled them, and gave them to a woman to ease labor. "In preparing this medicine the fronds of the fern were stripped from the stalk with a downward motion toward the roots and a prayer was offered that the child would 'slip' as easily as the fronds of the fern were removed."[24]

Adiantum pedatum L., var. **aleuticum** Rupr. Maidenhair Fern.

Green River	tsa′btsub[25]
Lummi	tungwĕltcin, "hair medicine"
Makah	tlotlotc′sa′dit, "dry fern"[26]
Quileute	ha-pal-pulth *or* hah-polk-pulth[27]
Skokomish	aiya′o′lgad, "hair bigger"

Materials. The midrib of this fern, outstanding for its shiny dark brown surface, is used for the design in basketry by the Makah and Quinault. Reagan mentions no use but points out that the plant is common to shady places in rocky areas along the coast and elsewhere.[28]

Medicine. The leaves are soaked in water by the Makah, Lummi, and Skokomish, and this is used on the hair. The Makah chew the leaves for sore chest and stomach trouble. The leaves are chewed to check internal hemorrhages from wounds and therefore are valuable on the war path.[29] The Quinault burn the leaves and rub the ashes on the hair. This is just one of the many aids toward achieving long, shiny, black hair.

Pteridium aquilinum (L.) Kuhn, var. **lanuginosum** (Bong.) Fern. (*P. aquilinum*, var. *pubescens* Underw.) Brake Fern.

Chehalis	pat′a′kwaᵘnl; s′a′q, roots
Cowlitz	tc′a′latca, upper part; tc′a′kum, rhizome
Green River	tca′laca′ts; t′a′di, rhizome[30]
Klallam	tsĭcĭ′ĭtc
Lummi	skuxwɛn
Makah	sikla′buṗt; sik!la′, rhizomes
Quileute	k′aqwa′ap′ut,[31] whole plant; k′aqwe, rhizome
	laqwitsitsĕ′qwl, "wiping the fish," leaves
Quinault	tsumxe′xnix
Skagit	stca′lasets, whole plant; sqI′ūx, roots; saq′, roots
Skokomish	sa′akai
Snohomish	tca′lasats
Squaxin	tc′a′lacats
Swinomish	tc′a′lasats

Food. The rhizomes of this fern were just as intensively used as one might expect from its growth in western Washington. They were roasted in the ashes, peeled and the mealy center eaten to supply the starchy element in diet. This use is recorded for every group listed above as well as for the Lower Chinook.[32] The Cowlitz also eat the tops of the young plants raw. The Swinomish store baked rhizomes in baskets. The Lummi dig the roots after the weather turns cold. The Skagit dig ferns at Birdsview and select only those that ooze juice. The Skokomish also get the roots in the fall.

Materials. The Makah, Quileute, Squaxin, and Swinomish use the leaves to lay fish on while cleaning it and to wipe the fish. The Squaxin use the leaves for camp bedding. According to one informant the Quinault use the fibers in the rhizomes for making string, but no confirmation of this statement was secured.

[19] Ballard.
[20] Haeberlin and Gunther, p. 20.
[21] Olson, p. 53.
[22] Densmore, p. 317.
[23] Olson, p. 53.
[24] Densmore, p. 317.
[25] Steve Sam through Ballard.
[26] The Makah name given by Densmore, p. 311, is kloko′sasud, "leaves wither quickly."
[27] Reagan, p. 56.
[28] *Loc. cit.*
[29] Densmore, pp. 313, 316.
[30] Ballard.
[31] kakwa-put, kah-a-kwa, hkak-kwah-put: Reagan, p. 56.
[32] Ray, p. 120.

Literature. Mr. Reagan states that this fern can be found especially in burnt-over places and that the Indians, meaning the Quileute, burned over Forks and Quillayute prairie in order to lure elk and deer to feed on the young fern shoots.[33] Jones mentions Quillayute Prairie as having a particularly luxuriant growth of brake.[34] Reagan describes a fern-paste bread made by the Indians from the pounded and dried pulp of the rhizomes of this fern but adds that he never saw any. The wide use of this fern attracted the attention of such early travelers as Lewis and Clark[35] and Swan.[36]

Struthiopteris spicant (L.) Weis.   Deer Fern.

Makah	i'i'ts'bak'kuk[37]
Quileute	kĕstola'put
Quinault	ska'ĕ'ĕtskɫ'o

Food. This fern is used only in emergency. The Quileute tell a child to look for it when he is lost and eat the root. The leaves are eaten by Makah when traveling to prevent thirst.[38]

Materials. The Quinault used these leaves with sword fern to cook baking camas.

Medicine. The leaves of this fern were boiled and the liquid drunk for general ill health by the Quileute, but they also put the fresh leaves on paralyzed parts of the body. The Quinault chewed the young leaves raw for colic. The Makah eat the green leaves for lung trouble or distress in the stomach.[39]

There is no reference to deer fern among modern medical usages.

Miscellaneous. The Cowlitz informant had no name for the plant and said it was not used.

EQUISETACEAE

Equisetum. Horsetail, Scouring-rush. The horsetails are being grouped together for discussion because they are so often put to the same uses. In some cases when only one variety was discussed it is an open question as to whether the informant could have distinguished varieties.

Equisetum hyemale L.   Common Scouring-rush.

Cowlitz	sikwsi'k
Quileute	tselatc'ɫput
Quinault	mo xwin, "horses eat it"[40]
Skokomish	xwi'k'tud

Equisetum Telmateia Ehrh.   Giant Horsetail.

Cowlitz	smu q'; xumxu m, roots
Klallam	ma'ax
Makah	ba'axbupt

Quileute	tutu'tsi; to'to'tseput, "growing things"; ya'ksa, mature plant; tsĕ'xak, root
Quinault	tĕto'ts, "to eat it" (first sprouts); ska'atos, roots[41]
Swinomish	bu bxadts; bu· bx, "makes it smooth"

Equisetum arvense L.   Field Horsetail.

Food. Since the horsetails are among the first green sprouts in the early spring, it is natural that they should be sought as food by people whose vegetable diet through the winter is mainly dried. The stem of the early reproductive shoot of the *E. Telmateia* is peeled and eaten raw by the Klallam,[42] Makah, Quileute, and Quinault. The Lower Chinook use the young shoots of *E. arvense.* The Cowlitz dry the cone-like top of the stalk of *E. hyemale*, mash it and mix it with salmon eggs. Later in the season the little bulbs on the root stock of *E. Telmateia* are eaten after being cooked. This method is used by the Klallam, Makah, Cowlitz, Lower Chinook,[43] and Quinault,[44] who eat the root with whale or seal oil. Some also eat the bulbs raw as was cited for the Makah by Swan,[45] and noted by informants for the Cowlitz and Swinomish, and mentioned by Olson for the Quinault.[46] The Quileute do not use these bulbs as food.

Materials. The *E. hyemale* which is known as the scouring-rush was used by the Cowlitz and Quinault for polishing arrow shafts, while the Swinomish informant designated the *E. Telmateia* for the same purpose. The Skokomish use it with dogfish skin as sandpaper. After horses were introduced this rush was considered good fodder by the Quileute and called "horses eat it" by the Quinault. The Cowlitz use the black root for imbrication on the coiled basket, as do the Quileute and Swinomish.

Medicine. Quileute swimmers rub themselves with *E. hyemale* to feel strong. More specifically the Cowlitz break up the stalks of the same horsetail, boil them, and wash hair infested with vermin in this water. The Quinault, according to a woman informant, boil the stems of the scouring-rush with willow leaves and give the infusion to a girl whose menstrual period is not regular. The informant insisted that this was not used as a possible abortive. The Quinault press the juice out of the root of the giant horsetail and mix it with human milk and use it as a wash for sore eyes, or an infusion of the root alone is used.[47] The Makah eat the heads of the reproductive shoot raw as a cure for diarrhoea.

Literature. Reagan mentions the use of two scouring rushes, *E. hyemale* and *E laevigatum*, as food.[48]

[33] Reagan, p. 56.
[34] Jones, *Olympic Peninsula*, p. 91.
[35] Thwaites, vol. 4, p. 5; vol. 3, p. 362.
[36] Swan, *Northwest Coast*, p. 88.
[37] "Resembling another plant called i'itsba," meaning given by Densmore, p. 310.
[38] Densmore, p. 319.
[39] Densmore, p. 313.
[40] Olson, p. 53.

[41] Olson, p. 53.
[42] Gunther, p. 206.
[43] Ray, p. 120.
[44] Olson, p. 53.
[45] Swan, *Cape Flattery*, p. 25.
[46] Olson, p. 53.
[47] Olson, p. 180.
[48] Reagan, p. 57.

Jones points out that Reagan's identification of the latter is erroneous for it does not exist in western Washington.[49] For *laevigatum* he gives the following Quileute names: ba-ba wh, totstse, bah-ah'wh, and ba-ah'wh-tots-tse, leading one to believe that his falsely identified variety is probably *Telmateia*. He states that these horsetails are eaten ceremonially, a point which did not come out in discussing their use with the present informants.

The *Equisetaceae* as a family have little medicinal value according to Gathercoal and Wirth[50] and specifically *E. Telmateia* does not appear in the pharmacognosies consulted. The U. S. Dispensatory lists an infusion of the plant as being used sometimes in dropsical and renal diseases, a totally different use from any given above.

TAXACEAE. Yew Family

Taxus brevifolia Nutt. Western Yew.

Common especially along streams.[51]

Chehalis	k'ła·'mk'ł
Cowlitz	wawani'nc
Klallam	ǩlinka'łtc
Makah	k'lexedakxłebapt
Quinault	k'lam'ma'aq, "red wood"; tsē'ē'kak[52]
Samish	tliŋka'łtc
Snohomish	ts'xa'bēt
Swinomish	ts'xūbī'dats

Food. This tree furnishes no food, but the Klallam, Samish, and Swinomish dry the needles, pulverize them and use them in place of tobacco for smoking. The Snohomish mixed them with kinnikinnick and later with tobacco.

Materials. The wood of the yew is considered very valuable and used for weapons and implements that require strength and toughness. It is specifically mentioned for bows and arrows by the Snohomish, Swinomish, Samish, Chehalis, Klallam, Makah, Quinault. The shaft of the whale harpoon is made of yew by the Makah according both to a present-day informant and the observations of Swan.[53] The shafts of all harpoons—salmon, seal, and porpoise— are made of yew by the Quinault, Samish, and Swinomish. The same tribes also use yew for the framework at the mouth of the dip net. The framework is called spo"otun tc'ots'a'ixᵘ by the Quinault. Canoe paddles are made of yew by the Klallam, Makah, and Quinault who call them xwa·'pi.[54] Further fishing and canoe equipment made of yew consists of the canoe bailer (lixᵘtcutu'nh) of the Quinault and their club for killing the sea-lion and the fur seal as well as the clubs of the Samish and Swinomish. The Swino-

mish also use yew for war clubs. Wedges used in splitting logs are made of yew by the Cowlitz, Samish, and Swinomish. The digging stick used for roots and clams, since it must be tough, is made of yew by the Quinault, Swinomish, and the Cowlitz. In household utensils yew is also favored for the carving of spoons and dishes by the Makah, of spoons by the Quinault. The Makah make trinket boxes of yew which are square, burnt out of one piece, and have lids. Combs are also carved of yew by the Cowlitz and Quinault. Recognizing the same springiness which makes yew so desirable for bows, the Cowlitz also use it for the frame of the drum. In addition to these many uses Olson also mentions the spring pole of the Quinault deer trap as being made of yew.[55]

Medicine. Just as the wood of the yew is used where strength is required, so the tree is also used medicinally to impart strength. Smooth sticks of yew are used by a Swinomish youth to rub himself to gain strength. The Swinomish use boughs to rub themselves when bathing. The Chehalis crush the leaves and soak them in water which is used to bathe a baby or an old person. It is supposed to make them perspire and improve their condition. While the Chehalis never drink this water, the Klallam prepare leaves in the same way, boil them, and drink the infusion for any internal injury or pain. The Cowlitz moisten leaves of yew, grind them up, and apply the pulp to wounds. The Quinault chew the leaves and spit them on wounds. This stings, but is supposed to be very healing. They are the only tribe making medicinal use of the bark, which is peeled, dried, and boiled. The liquid is drunk as lung medicine.

Literature. There is no mention of yew in any of the pharmacognosies consulted; but it is stated that it has been analyzed and no alkaloids were found.[56] The tree is discussed by Reagan, who states that the name for it among the Hoh and Quileute is he-yah or he-ah. In addition to the uses listed above, he mentions the discs for their games, probably meaning the disc game called slahalem by most of the Salish. Reagan also states that this tree is important in the mythology of this region.[57] Since no information on the yew was secured from the modern Quileute, these statements could not be checked.

PINACEAE. Pine Family

Pinus monticola Dougl. Western White Pine.

This tree occurs from sea level to an altitude of 5,000 feet.[58]

Lummi	q'woxtcł, q'woxwutcł
Quinault	tå'tskanil[59]
Skagit	sa'akū'sats

---

[49] Jones, *Olympic Peninsula*, p. 92.
[50] Gathercoal and Wirth, p. 71.
[51] Jones, *Olympic Peninsula*, p. 94.
[52] Given by another informant who said it also meant red wood. This has not been checked. The other word was given by two informants.
[53] Swan, *Cape Flattery*, p. 20.
[54] Also cited in Olson, p. 71.
[55] *Ibid.*, p. 51.
[56] Muenscher, p. 29.
[57] Reagan, p. 57.
[58] Jones, *Olympic Peninsula*, p. 95.
[59] Olson, p. 181. Not from an identified specimen.

Materials. The husband of my Skagit informant volunteered the information that light dugouts of pine were used on the river by the Upper Skagit, but they were rare. This is the only use of this tree for any purpose except medicinal.

Medicine. The Quinault boil the bark and drink the infusion for disorders of the stomach and to purify the blood. This same medicine is used by the Lummi and Skagit for tuberculosis, while the Skagit also use it for cuts and sores; but they insist that it be boiled, for unboiled it would draw a sore together too quickly. The very young shoots of the pine are boiled, and a Skagit suffering from rheumatism is bathed in the water. My informant states that a man had been cured in this way just a few years ago.

Both the Lummi and the Skagit chew the pitch-like gum.

Literature. Pinus albus and *P. Strabus* are listed by Youngken as being used in preparations for cough medicine.[60] Reagan mentions that the Hoh and Quileute chew pine gum for pleasure and for coughs.[61]

Pinus contorta Dougl. Lodgepole Pine.

Common in swampy ground near the ocean coast; also on the gravelly prairies on the southern end of the Olympic Peninsula.[62]

Quinault ha"agwał[63]; t'atnixło

Medicine. The pitch is put on an open sore. The buds are chewed for a sore throat.

Picea sitchensis (Bong.) Carr. Sitka Spruce.

Chiefly from sea level to less than 1,000 feet elevation, usually in alluvial soil, most abundant along the ocean coast.[64]

Hoh and Quileute	yak-tsu[65]
Makah	k!ło'pate, tree; k!pak'kě'dibis, gum
Quileute	ya'ksa, "sharp needles"; tili"it, roots, "good splitters" (referring to roots for basketry)
Quinault	sulu'x, tree; kwa'aleł[66]; k'wulx̣ʷ, "little limbs," referring to the needles of any conifer
Swinomish	ts'alka'yats, "sharp ends"[67]

Food. Only the Makah use any part of the spruce tree as food and they eat the young shoots raw. Both they and the Quinault chew the pitch as gum for pleasure, the Quinault warming theirs before using it.[68] While the Quileute use no part of the spruce as food for themselves, they recognize the fact that squirrels feed on the cones.

Materials. Many uses are made of the Sitka Spruce. Starting with the root: this is used for basketry by all of the tribes on the Pacific Coast in this area, in contrast to the use of cedar roots in the Puget Sound area and toward the Cascades. The use of spruce root for baskets and rain hats is given specifically by the Makah,[69] Quinault,[70] and Quileute. The Quinault also used the roots for tying the tines of the salmon spear,[71] as did the Quileute. The Quinault sewed the corners of boxes with spruce root,[72] according to Olson, but Billy Garfield and Alice Jackson told Mr. Ernesti that the limbs were used for whaling rope, to tie house parts together, and to tie in the cross pieces in canoes; and the question arises whether it was not possibly the withe of limbs that was used on the boxes as was the practice farther north, among the Kwakiutl for example.

The pitch of the spruce is used for caulking canoes by the Quileute and Quinault, and the Makah also used it for protecting the harpoon point. For this purpose it is usually applied warm. The Quileute use a spruce sapling for the spring pole of a snare for deer, elk, or any other game animal.

Medicine. The Makah burn the bark of the spruce together with that of wild cherry (*Prunus emarginata*) and the charcoal powder is put on an infant's navel when the cord comes off. The Quinault make a tea of the young inside bark and drink it for a "tickling throat," or they chew the bark and swallow the saliva. The Quinault apply the gum to cuts and wounds.[73] Less specifically medicinal in its use is the rubbing of the body with spruce boughs while bathing, which is done by the Makah. Furthermore, according to Densmore a decoction is used to "take out bad blood" and as a strengthening bath.[74]

Charms. A Makah whaler may stick a sprig of spruce into his hair knot when he goes to sea, according to Swan.[75]

Literature. Reagan lists the spruce as *Picea Engelmanni* Parry, which Jones believes is an erroneous identification.[76] Reagan mentions the use of spruce for shakes, clapboards, puncheon-planks, and toys and says that spruce limbs and roots are shredded, pounded, and then twisted into cord and rope.[77]

Spruce is not mentioned in the National Formulary, Bastedo, Norton, or U. S. Dispensatory.

Tsuga heterophylla (Raf.) Sarg. Hemlock.

Occurs from sea level to 3,000 feet elevation.[78]

Cowlitz	sisku'pas
Klallam	sqwěto'sī"ěltc

[60] Youngken, pp. 96, 97.
[61] Reagan, p. 58.
[62] Jones, *Olympic Peninsula*, p. 95.
[63] This name was given to Mr. Ernesti by Billy Garfield. Mrs. Cole, my informant, said that this means White Pine (*Pinus monticola*), and gave me the alternate word listed above.
[64] Jones, *Olympic Peninsula*, p. 95.
[65] Reagan, p. 59.
[66] Olson, p. 180.
[67] The Swinomish do not use spruce, and say that at present it is very scarce on their reservation.
[68] Olson, p. 60, as well as present informant.

[69] Swan, *Cape Flattery*, p. 16.
[70] Olson, p. 55.
[71] *Ibid.*, p. 69, as well as present informants.
[72] *Ibid.*, p. 80.
[73] *Ibid.*, p. 180.
[74] Densmore, pp. 313, 318.
[75] Swan, *Cape Flattery*, p. 17.
[76] Jones, *Olympic Peninsula*, p. 95.
[77] Reagan, p. 59.
[78] Jones, *Olympic Peninsula*, p. 96.

Lummi	sqwa′kunītcɫ
Makah	klak!a′bupt; tkaka′bup;[79] tkatka′-bup[80]
Quileute	ti·′la;[81] te-e-thlu[82]
Quinault	kᵘhwa′lp, tree; kuma′ktun, bark
Skagit	t!k!ad′ı
Snohomish	t!kadı′
Swinomish	t!ɛdk!adı′

Food. No part of the hemlock tree is used as food in this area; only the Cowlitz use the small tips of the branches as flavor when cooking bear meat. The inner bark is not eaten here as among the Northern Athapascan.

Materials. Bark: The Klallam, Lummi,[83] and Makah boil the bark for a red-brown dye. The Makah, according to Densmore, prepare the dye in the following way: The inner bark was pounded and boiled in salt water. This made a reddish paint that was applied to spears and similar articles, and seemed to preserve wood. Some believed that a painted paddle lasted longer if held over a fire, thus baking the paint.[84] The Snohomish use this dye for baskets. The Chehalis use the dye on fish nets to make them invisible to the fish;[85] furthermore, the smell of this dye attracts the salmon. The Quileute chop the bark fine, boil it, and apply the juice to spruce-root baskets to make them water-tight. The Quileute also use the bark in tanning hides. The Quinault mash the bark and salmon eggs to get a yellow-orange paint for dip nets and paddles. The Quinault soak the bark, shape it, and sew it to form a lining for the cooking pit,[86] and also use it as a storage container for elderberries.[87]

Boughs: The Quinault use boughs as shelters for hunters. The Makah sink hemlock boughs in the water to collect herring eggs, a use not current among the Quinault, for they do not eat the spawn.[88]

Young trees are used by the Quinault, Skagit, and Snohomish for poling canoes upstream. They are also used for the walk along the top of a fish weir by the Quinault, while the Klallam use the saplings as stanchions of a fish trap strung across a stream. The Skagit also use young hemlocks in fish-trap construction, while the Lummi use them as poles for large dip nets.

The wood of the hemlock is used largely for firewood and is especially mentioned for this purpose by the Quinault and Chehalis. The Cowlitz do not use hemlock for combs and the Quinault informants contradict each other on this use. Olson records it,[89] while Billy Garfield, Mr. Ernesti's informant, denied it.

Medicine. The pitch of the hemlock is a favorite preparation to use on the face, both as paint and to prevent chapping. The Quinault mix pitch with ground hemlock bark and make dark brown face paint (sdja′·muts). This is also applied to a child's chest as a cure for a cold. The pitch alone is used by the Cowlitz to prevent chapping and by the Makah to prevent sunburn. The Quinault also mix the pitch with the marrow from an elk tibia and rub it on eyebrows to make them beautiful.[90] The Makah put the pitch on the hair to remove vermin, and, according to Densmore, also use the powdered bark mixed with oil for the same purpose.[91] The bark of the hemlock is frequently used medicinally. The Quinault boil it for a laxative, while the same infusion is used by the Cowlitz and Skagit as a wash for sore eyes or sores on the skin. According to them, bark tea will also stop a hemorrhage. To make it more effective the Klallam add licorice fern to stop hemorrhages. The Chehalis pound the bark and boil it in order to use the tea for syphilis and tuberculosis. The Skagit use the same bark tea for sore throat. According to Swan, the bark is chewed by the Makah and applied to a wound to stop bleeding, and the bark of the roots is dried, rubbed on a stone with saliva, and applied to· the face.[92] According to Densmore, a growth of bark forms on the wound of the tree; this is dipped in water, rubbed on a rock, and used as a poultice for an obstinate sore.[93] The young tips of the hemlock are chewed and spit on a swelling to reduce it, by the Quileute. These same tips the Klallam boil, and drink the infusion to cure tuberculosis and to stimulate appetite.

Finally, the Quinault braid hemlock and rub themselves with this during bathing while in training.[94]

A decoction of hemlock, part not named, is drunk hot for internal injury, by the Makah.[95]

Charms. The Quinault hollow out a small log of hemlock, fill it with small objects, decorate it, and manipulate it to cause a storm by magic.[96]

Literature. Reagan has hemlock listed under two varieties, the one given above and also *T. mertensiana* (Bong.) Sarg., which Jones classifies as principally a timberline tree. There was no opportunity of finding a specimen of this. Reagan does not indicate that the Indians distinguished between them. He states that the trees were used medicinally, specifically mentioning the bark as an emetic, a use not given by the modern Quileute. The use of bark for tanning is, however, corroborated.[97]

The tree is not mentioned in any of the pharmaceutical books.

---

[79] Densmore, p. 311.
[80] *Ibid.*, p. 316.
[81] Andrade, p. 189.
[82] Reagan, p. 58.
[83] Stern, p. 89.
[84] Densmore, p. 320.
[85] See *Pseudotsuga taxifolia* (Douglas Fir)—"Materials."
[86] Olson, p. 40.
[87] *Ibid.*, pp. 54, 80.
[88] *Ibid.*, p. 84.
[89] *Ibid.*, p. 60.

[90] *Ibid.*, p. 61.
[91] Densmore, p. 316.
[92] Swan, *Cape Flattery*, pp. 78, 18.
[93] Densmore, p. 316.
[94] Olson, p. 143.
[95] Densmore, p. 318.
[96] Olson, p. 165.
[97] Reagan, p. 58.

Abies grandis Lindl. White Fir.

Usually in moist situations, associated with Douglas fir and western red cedar; apparently very scarce near the ocean coast.[98] Only a few specimens of this variety of fir were identified. Whether they were overlooked in other places is uncertain, but informants seemed satisfied with only one kind of fir.

Chehalis   t'awi't·tł
Green River   łuqtci'ats

The only use the Chehalis have for this wood is for fuel. The same informant identified both this specimen and one of Douglas fir. The Green River information was secured from Mr. Ballard, who commented on that fact that his informants also distinguished between this fir and the Douglas fir. The needles of this variety were boiled as a tea for colds. On the other hand, the Swinomish informant insisted that this variety was the same as the Douglas and assured Mr. Ernesti that it looked different because of its environment.

Pseudotsuga taxifolia (Lamb.) Britt. (*Pseudotsuga mucronata* (Raf.) Sudw.) Douglas Fir.

This is the most abundant tree on the Olympic Peninsula and is common up to 3,500 feet in the Cascade range.[99]

Chehalis	t'camo·'ma, "evergreen family" pa'yu'tspaytł, "squirrels eat them," cones
Cowlitz	ta'xsa, big tree; ta'xsata'xsa, little tree
Green River	tcībe̅'dats[100]
Klallam	tcī'a'tcīltc
Lummi	tce̅'e̅'sun
Quileute	klay-hayts, klay-nayts[101]
Quinault	dja'·mats, whole tree
Skagit	stcūbī'dats, large tree; skoqwa'-batsets, small tree; spe̅polqˣ, cone
Snohomish	łu'kta'·tciyats,[102] "needles are wide"; łu'kłu'kta·'tciyats, "boughs"
Squaxin	qu'xbi
Swinomish	squ'biyaqsa·'ts

Food. Since the pitch was not chewed primarily as a medicine, it is listed here, though with some hesitation. The Klallam and Cowlitz chewed it like gum and so did the Quinault, according to Olson,[103] but this is denied by Garfield, Ernesti's informant.

Materials. Fir is most important as firewood, and, since its gathering requires less work, the bark is even more eagerly sought. This use is mentioned by the Quinault, Cowlitz, Skagit, Lummi, Klallam, Swinomish, Chehalis, and Green River. The Quin-

ault also make torches of the pitchy parts.[104] Since fir does not split evenly, it is not used for woodwork, but serves well as shafts for harpoons, salmon spears, and handles of dip nets. The Quinault use it for all these purposes. The spear and harpoon shafts are made of it by the Cowlitz, Skagit, Lummi, Klallam, Swinomish, Chehalis, and Green River. The boughs of the fir are used in the sweat lodge, being put over the hot rocks by the Swinomish.[105] The bark is boiled by the Swinomish to make a light brown dye which is used on fish nets to make them invisible to the fish.[106]

Medicine. The pitch of the fir is put on sores by the Cowlitz, Quinault, and the Skagit. It is boiled and drunk as a cold medicine by the Cowlitz and Squaxin, who also mix the needles with cedar, to make a tea for colds. The Swinomish boil fir needles alone for a general tonic tea, which they also heat and apply to the chest to "draw out the pain." The bark is boiled by the Skagit as an antiseptic—the informant telling of this remedy was using it on a badly infected finger. The bark of young roots is boiled by the Swinomish and drunk as tea for colds, and babies are washed in it. The bud tips are also picked by them and chewed for sore throat or sores in the mouth.

Charms. The cones of fir are thought to have magic quality in several tribes. The Chehalis warm them by the fire so the rain will stop. The Cowlitz put them close to the fire with a prayer for sunshine. The Skagit say that when salt-water people are marooned on account of wind, they burn cones and point the boat in the direction from which they wish the wind to come.

Literature. Reagan mentions for the Hoh and Quileute that the wood is used for fuel and for making shakes and clapboards, a practice which is post-white.

Thuja plicata Donn. Western Red Cedar.

Abundant from sea level to about 3,000 feet elevation.[107]

Chehalis	łata'wi; p'alans
Cowlitz	nuŋk, tree; lot'sa'kes, cedar bark; pa'lumkwi, shredded cedar bark
Klallam	xatca'tcł
Lummi	x'pai'epł, whole tree; x'pai, buds; slōwe̅', bark
Makah	pī'ts·ŏp, bark, dried but not broken
Quileute	t'sa'p·is, whole tree; t'sa·'t'apis, plural[108] t'sapi'stat, branches; ya'ksa, long straight branches used for rope; t'sapi'stcit, cedar bark on tree; si'k'u'ya, bark peeled off

[98] Jones, *Olympic Peninsula*, p. 96.
[99] *Ibid.*, p. 97.
[100] Ballard.
[101] Reagan, p. 58.
[102] tcubi'dats given by Mrs. Shelton. The above given by an informant in Swinomish territory as being Snohomish.
[103] Olson, p. 60.

[104] *Ibid.*, p. 77.
[105] Stuhr (No. 324) mentions the use of the leaves by the Indians in sweat baths to cure rheumatism and it is unfortunate that no source is given for this information.
[106] See *Tsuga heterophylla* (Hemlock)—"Materials: bark."
[107] Jones, *Olympic Peninsula*, p. 97.
[108] Andrade, *Handbook*, pt. 3, p. 189.

Quinault   t'ci·'tum, whole tree; t'ci·'tumcila'c, limb; k'wiloɬ, bark

Skagit   xaxpai''ats, tree; sɬuxwai, bark

Skokomish   q!wĕ'le

Snohomish   xeɬpai'its

Squaxin   χpa'yats

Swinomish   xĕxpai''ĕs, tree; xĕxpai'tcɬ, bough of cedar

Materials. Throughout the whole Northwest the wood most extensively used by the Indians is cedar. House planks, house posts, roof boards, and canoes are made exclusively of this wood. Boxes, including those with bent sides. and dugouts are of cedar. Swan mentions that the Makah made cradles of cedar,[109] and a modern informant refers to its use for arrowshatts. The Quileute make the hearth of the fire drill of cedar, as well as the spindle for spinning mountain-goat wool. The Squaxin make the herring rake of cedar. The charcoal of cedar wood mixed with salmon eggs is used by the Quinault to rub on canoe paddles, which are held in pitch wood smoke and then rubbed with green grass to produce a lasting shiny black.

Equally as useful as the wood is the bark of the cedar tree, in fact there is no single item so ubiquitous in the Indian household. The shredding of bark is a constant bit of busy work for women, done by the Chehalis with a deer-bone chopper. It is shredded fine enough to be used as padding for infants' cradles, as sanitary pads, as towels. A coarser grade is plaited into skirts and capes, later into complete dresses for women. The Lower Chehalis use cedar bark for clothing, while the Upper Chehalis depend more on skins, a situation duplicated whenever a tribe is divided into a salt-water and an up-river group. Shredded bark is used for ceremonial head bands and for playing slahalem. In its unshredded state cedar bark is cut in strips of varying widths, the broader ones plaited to serve as dishes or as individual plates, as used by the Cowlitz, who also interweave cedar and maple to make larger platters. They also use cedar bark to line cooking pits. A small, coarse, twilled mat is used by several Puget Sound tribes for laying out boiled salmon. Canoe bailers are folded of large pieces of cedar bark and lashed with wild cherry bark. Wads of shredded cedar bark are used as tinder for fires and also carried in a slow torch on journeys.

The narrower strips are woven into mats by the Makah. The use of cedar bark for matting is much more prevalent to the north of this area, but the Makah make a few mats even though they much prefer to get them by trade from their Nootkan cousins. The Makah are the only coast tribe in Washington even to attempt to make them. The Quileute, like the Makah, also use the cedar mat as a sail, but in all probability they secured them through trading. The lining and head band of the rain hat were made of split cedar by the Quinault, Quileute, and Makah. The Quileute string dried clams and smelts for storage on strips of cedar bark. For many purposes cedar bark is dyed with alder juice to give it a rich red-brown color.

The limbs of the cedar tree are stripped of their leaves, soaked in water, and twisted into rope. The heavier grades are used by the whale-hunting tribes like the Quinault, Quileute, and Makah for towing home dead whales. It has remarkable strength. Single limbs which have been worked to pliability are used to tie or sew the corners of wooden boxes and tie cross pieces in canoes. The Quileute string pecten shells on a small cedar limb as a dance rattle. Cedar limbs are used for openwork baskets by the Quinault and Squaxin, and also for weaving with vine maple sticks for fish weirs, and by the Snuqualmi for tying the poles of the summer house.

The roots of the cedar tree are used widely, in both western and eastern Washington, for the coiled and imbricated basket. They are split fine and used for the foundation, then trimmed more carefully for the sewing element. The only part of this area where cedar is not used for basketry is on the Pacific coast from the Quinault northward, where spruce is substituted. In searching for roots for basketry, the Squaxin were anxious to get those lying under rotten logs. Roots are also used by the Quinault for sewing the corners of wooden boxes.

Medicine. The Lummi chew the buds of cedar and swallow them for sore lungs, while the Cowlitz chew them for toothache, and the Skokomish boil them for a gargle. The Skagit boil the ends of the leaves for coughs. The Cowlitz boil the tips and mix them with some roots, which the informant could not identify, for a cold medicine. The Klallam boil cedar limbs for tuberculosis medicine. The Chehalis peel the bark of a small tree, and the inner part is chewed or boiled and the liquid drunk to help bring about menstruation. The informant stressed the fact that this was not used in case pregnancy was suspected, but only if there was a delay in menstruation. The Quinault make an infusion of the bark and twigs for kidney trouble.[110] The seeds of cedar are steeped with the ends of the limbs and the infusion drunk to break a fever. The Quinault boil an infusion of cedar limbs to wash sores due to venereal diseases.

In addition to these medicinal uses, the leaves and limbs of cedar are used for scouring the body in bathing, both for ordinary purposes and in preparation for ceremonial occasions. This was mentioned by Swan[111] and also by present-day informants. Among the Lummi, a boy takes the boughs he has used to rub himself before a guardian spirit quest and fastens them to the top of a cedar tree. Whalers put piles of cedar branches under their beds to make themselves ready for the hunt and to ward off bad luck.

---

[109] Swan, *Cape Flattery*, p. 18.

[110] Olson, p. 181.
[111] Swan, *Cape Flattery*, p. 19.

There is a strong association between cedar and death. Lummi men, burying a corpse, chew cedar tips to avoid nausea. Cedar limbs, singed, were used by the Lummi as a broom to sweep off the walls of a house after the removal of the corpse. The Skagit burned cedar limbs at night and waved them through the house to scare the ghost after death.

The handles of the dip net used between two canoes are struck with cedar boughs to remove the odor of fish.

In this discussion of cedar tribal names are not always mentioned, because the use of the tree is so universal that a few names used might only be misleading. The instances given are just specific examples.

Literature. Reagan has a long discussion of cedar for which he gives as the Hoh and Quileute word, "to-dilth," a word hard to equate with t'sa'p is. He speaks especially of the use of cedar for the making of canoes, ranging from the little river canoe to the ocean-going one which will hold ten whalers or three tons of freight. He says, "A canoe for ocean use is now worth about $200." Although his paper was published in 1934, I think the data for it were gathered some years ago.[112]

In 1792 Menzies spoke in his journal of "mats made of bark of trees used for house coverings" which he saw on the shores of the Gulf of Georgia on June 19th.[113] Probably these were mat-covered summer houses or fishing camps.

This tree is cited by Densmore as giant arborvitae with "general economic uses."[114] It is also in the general list as used for dye and medicine; however, its medicinal qualities are not specified, nor are the particulars given of its use as a dye.[115]

Juniperus scopulorum Sarg. Rocky Mountain Juniper.
Swinomish   i'yalats, "smells strong" (i'yal, smell)

Medicine. Roots are boiled and the infusion is used to bathe the feet as a cure for rheumatism. The leaves are boiled so the odor will disinfect the house, and a sick person is also bathed in the infusion for the same purpose. This infusion is also drunk as a general tonic.

Literature. Reagan states that the twigs and berries are used by the Quileute for ceremonies.[116]

J. communis is listed by Gathercoal and Wirth as diuretic.[117]

TYPHACEAE. Cat-tail Family

Typha latifolia L. Broad-leaved Cat-tail.
Chehalis   swalalt'cɪ'lc
Cowlitz   tstci'yux
Klallam   qwŏ''ot

112 Reagan, p. 58.
113 Menzies, p. 58.
114 Densmore, p. 321.
115 *Ibid.*, p. 308.
116 Reagan, p. 57.
117 Gathercoal and Wirth, p. 95.

Makah   salaxa'xbupt; sala'xax, "mat"
Quinault   sgwitci'; kwilgo''s, top of stalk
Snohomish   ŏ'lal; kɛsū'b, string made of leaf
Squaxin   o'lal

Food. The Chehalis bake the roots and inner stalks in the ashes for eating. The roots are eaten raw by the Lower Chinook.[118]

Materials. The cat-tail is much more widely used for mat making than as food. Even where the use of cat-tails is not listed here, there is reasonable surety that they were used. At Neah Bay the Makah state that cat-tails have always been very scarce, and their gathering necessitates some travel from their villages. The Makah call the fruiting stalk "the wife" and use it for mats, while the male stalk, called "tcacu'p," is never used. The Quinault also must travel for cat-tails, going to Grays Harbor to get them in quantity. Mats are made of the fruiting stalks by all the groups listed above and, as stated before, probably by most tribes in western Washington. The mats are used as hangings and screens inside the winter houses and as coverings for temporary houses and shelters in the summer. The latter use is found everywhere except among the Makah. Mats are also used as mattresses and it is amazing how springy a new mat can be. Kneeling pads in canoes are of cat-tail mats, as are raincoats and capes. The Quinault make large wallet-like packsacks of cat-tails. A light-weight basket is made in an openwork crossed-warp twine using cat-tails. The Snohomish also use the leaves, carefully peeled, for making a two-ply string which is rolled on the bare thigh. This string is used for sewing the mats. The Chehalis use the edges of the leaves for imbrication on coiled baskets.

NAIADACEAE. Pondweed Family

Phyllospadix Scouleri Hook. Surf-grass.
Makah   xūxwa'p
Quileute   xa·'k'

Food. In the spring the Makah eat the roots of this grass raw.

Materials. A bunch of this grass is used as a target for arrow practice by Quileute boys. It is tough and durable but is never used for basketry.

GRAMINEAE. Grass Family

Elymus mollis Trin. (*E. arenarius* Piper, not L.) Rye-grass.
Makah   tcupxa'bupt
Quileute   k'a'k'ɵput, "strong"

Materials. Bundles of rye-grass roots are used by the Makah to rub the body after bathing. The Quileute braid the roots and tie them into bundles for the same purpose, calling them "twa'tsatixl." The Quinault lay the leaves thickly under salal berries

118 Ray, p. 121; also recorded by Swan, *Northwest Coast*, p. 88.

while they are drying. Although not identified from a specimen, it is probable that this is the grass the Quinault use for braiding tumplines.[119]

CYPERACEAE. Sedge Family

Carex (sitchensis?)[120] Basket Sedge.

It is used by the Makah for the bottom of trinket baskets.

Eriophorum Chamissonis C. A. Mey. Cotton Sedge.

Makah   popoxsa'dix, "feather plant"

Any plant with down is called "feather plant," the same name being applied to fireweed. It is not used. The specimen identified above and one found in a cranberry bog at Spruce Orchard are the only ones known to Dr. Jones from the Olympic Peninsula. The Quinault informant did not recognize it.

Scirpus acutus Muhl. (*S. occidentalis* (Wats.) Chase.) Tule.

Klallam	tsa'na'ux
Makah	t!ɑ'daxbupt
Snohomish	sqwɪqwa'ds

Materials. The Makah get tule at Lake Ozette and use it for making mats similar to cat-tail mats. The Quinault make packsacks and coarse baskets of tule.[121] The Klallam get tule in small ponds and use it for mats. The Snohomish gather tule in the fall and use it for mats.

ARACEAE. Arum Family

Lysichitum americanum Hulten and St. John. (*L. camtschatcense* of authors.) Skunk cabbage.

Cowlitz	ka'ilet, whole plant; dipdi·'p, seed stalk
Klallam	stco'qwe
Makah	tibu't[122]
Quileute	t'ŏ'qwa, "it smells," whole plant; t'ŏ'qwa'akĕ"itsa, seed stalk; t'ŏ'qwa'a'tsuboκł, root
Quinault	tsūlĕ'lŏs, "digging the roots"
Samish	t'ca·'uk'ʷ
Swinomish	t'cu·'k'ʷ

Food. The Quileute cook and eat the root as do the Lower Chinook,[123] who boil it for eating, but they do not prize it highly. The white part of the stalk below the ground is roasted on hot rocks by the Quinault in preparation for eating.[124] The Cowlitz stack the blossoms alternately along the sides of a stick, bury it and build a fire on top overnight. Then two or three are eaten; they are so strong that more

would make one sick. The Quileute say that bears enjoy skunk cabbage roots. The Skokomish steam the young leaves.

Materials. The leaves of skunk cabbage are used by the Quileute to wrap salal and elder berries while drying. The Samish and Swinomish double or roll the large leaves to make a cup for drinking or for picking berries. The Makah also use the leaves for drying salal berries and line berry baskets with them.

Medicine. The root is used in many ways, from infusions in which invalids are bathed by the Samish and Swinomish, to the chewing of the raw root by Makah women to effect an abortion. The Quinault boil the root and drink the liquid to clean out the bladder, while the Makah use the same concoction as a blood purifier. Densmore furthermore states that the Makah chew a little of the root to soothe the stomach after an emetic of red elderberry. It is hot like pepper.[125] Because of its supposed uterine action, the Quileute pound the root, boil it, and drink the juice to bring about easy delivery. The Klallam bake the root like bread and lay it on a carbuncle. The informant successfully used this on a carbuncle on his ankle.

The properties of the leaves, especially as a poultice, are known to many groups. The Quileute and Skokomish apply them to cuts and swellings, because they have a soothing effect; for the same reason they are used for headaches and fevers. The Makah warm the leaves and apply them to the chest for pain. The Quinault use the leaves as a general poultice. The Klallam hold the softest part of the leaf close to the fire and work it soft in the hands and put it on parts of the body sore with scrofula. The Cowlitz heat the blossom and apply it to the body for rheumatism. The Skokomish soak the roots in water and use it as a physic.

Charms. A Quileute sealer puts some leaves under the bow piece of his canoe because the leaves are dead and flat and will lie still, therefore the seal will lie still too and be caught easily. If a sealer took elk meat in his lunch, the seal would jump around because the elk is a "jumping" animal. Eggs in a lunch cause the seal to roll around in the water.

Literature. Reagan has the following information for the Quileute: when roasting camas, wild onion, and garlic, the Indians cover them with layers of skunk cabbage leaves, saying that they give the food a fine flavor. They wrap elderberries ready to be stored in these leaves, He also mentions the eating of roots by bears.[126] Haskins states that the use of skunk cabbage roots often saved coast Indian populations from starvation. The roots were supposedly cooked in pits, together with scrapings of the tender inner bark of hemlock, a method not described by any Indians of western Washington. But since Haskins does not give tribal names, it is impossible

---

[119] Olson, p. 88.
[120] At the time this book was first published (1945), sedges had not been accurately classified. This has since been done, but without a specimen it is impossible to use the new, extended classification.
[121] Olson, p. 84.
[122] Densmore, p. 311.
[123] Ray, p. 121; Swan, *Northwest Coast*, p. 87, "root, boiled and partially deprived of its acrid properties, is eaten"; Boas, p. 231.
[124] Olson, p. 54.

[125] Densmore, p. 314.
[126] Reagan, p. 59.

to check any of the information. The fondness of bears, and elk as well, for the roots is also mentioned by Haskins, who states that these animals often plowed up whole swamps to get them.

The Kathlamet Indians have an interesting myth concerning the skunk cabbage. In the ancient days, they say, there were no salmon. The Indians had nothing to eat save roots and leaves. Principal among these was the skunk cabbage. Finally the spring salmon came for the first time. As they passed up the river a person stood upon the shore and shouted: "Here come our relatives whose bodies are full of eggs. If it had not been for me all the people would have starved."

"Who speaks to us?" asked the salmon.
"Your uncle, skunk cabbage," was the reply.

Then the salmon went ashore to see him, and as a reward for having fed the people he was given an elk-skin blanket and a war club, and was set in the rich, soft soil near the river. There he stands to this day wrapped in his elk-skin blanket and holding aloft his war club.[127]

Stuhr states that the root forms the chief ingredient of the patent medicine "Skookum." It is reputed to be a stimulant, antispasmodic, and emetic for bronchial and pulmonary affections. It is used in a salve for ringworm, swellings, and inflammatory rheumatism.[128]

JUNCACEAE. Rush Family

Juncus effusus L. (*J. effusus hesperius* Piper.) Rush.

Quinault	k'lo"om, "grass"
	dja'lalcniɫ

There is some confusion in the Quinault information, but it is offered for what it is worth. It was obtained by the same field worker from a man and a woman. The former gave the first name and said it is used for plaiting tumplines for baskets. The woman gave the second name and said it is mixed with cat-tails to make string but not used for tumplines. She said that k'lo"om is larger and is used for tumplines. It has been impossible to check this conflicting information.

The Snuqualmi informant stated that the stalks are used for tying things but not for tumplines. Early sprouts of the larger plants are sometimes eaten raw.

Juncus xiphioides E. Mey., var. *triandrus* Engelm (*J. ensifolius* Wiks.)

Swinomish	skuba'laxkad

The information was obtained from the same informant for both the Swinomish and Samish tribes. He did not know the Samish name for the plant; he was sure that it did not grow in Samish territory. The Swinomish, he said, ate the bulb.

Literature. Reagan states that the Quileute used it as medicine.[129] *Juncoides* sp., with the common name of wood rush, is listed by Densmore for the Makah as kloklo' tcibakok, meaning "it looks like the green dye plant." The tender new shoots were given a barren woman to chew as an aid to fertility.[130]

LILIACEAE. Lily Family

Xerophyllum tenax (Pursh) Nutt. Pine Lily.

Chehalis	em[131]
Cowlitz	ya'i
Klallam	kɫakɫ
Quinault	k'ula·'ɫstap

Material. This plant, variously called bear grass, squaw grass, deer grass, or pine lily, as noted above, is used by all Indian groups in this territory.[132] It grows chiefly in the Hudsonian zone and was not readily available for identification, except when some of it was found dried or as it could be pointed to in a basket. It has only one use in the whole area, namely for overlay or decoration on basketry. Trimmed and tied in small bundles, the grass-like basal leaves of this plant make a welcome gift and a good article of trade.

Literature. Haskins mentions that at the Columbia Rapids there is much trade in *Xerophyllum*.[133]

Zigadenus venenosus Wats. Death Camas.

Chehalis	o'p' *or* u'p'
Squaxin	ba'q'a'

Both of these informants identified the plant from the same specimen, the only one found during these studies. It is regarded as a violent emetic and sometimes used as such, but on account of its poisonous nature is usually avoided. The Chehalis informant added that it belongs to the same family as camas.

Literature. Haskins states: "Indians were aware of its poisonous quality and were especially afraid because it grew where the other camas also flourished. The bulbs were powdered and applied as a poultice to cure boils, rheumatism, bruises, sprains, and to relieve pain. Unscrupulous medicine men were said to mix the root with a little tobacco and give it to a person to induce a severe nausea in order to receive a heavy fee for curing them."[134] It would be helpful to know to which tribe this statement applies.

In Menzies' Journal there is an entry at Birch Bay for June 12, 1792: "appeared to be a new species of melanthium," to which the editor added the marginal comment, "probably *Zygadenus venenosus* (poison camas)."[135]

127 Haskins, p. 5.
128 Stuhr, p. 17.
129 Reagan, p. 59.
130 Densmore, p. 317.
131 Adamson, MS Notes.
132 Since no specimen was found in Makah territory, it was neglected in this study but Miss Densmore, p. 320, records it as "Basket-grass from Taholah."
133 Haskins, p. 43.
134 Ibid., p. 33.
135 Menzies, p. 56.

This plant is also discussed at length by Muenscher, even the dried bulb[136] being described as very poisonous.

Veratrum Eschscholtzii Gray. (*V. viride* of Piper; *V. Eschscholtzianum* (R. & S.) Rydb.) False or Green Hellebore.

Cowlitz	mimu'n
Quinault	tcī'ai'nix

Medicine. This plant was secured only from two tribes with direct access to mountains. It belongs to the Hudsonian zone and among the Quinault is collected only up in the Spruce Orchard region. The Quinault boil the whole plant and drink it in very small doses for rheumatism. They regard it as poisonous. The Cowlitz are also aware of its poisonous qualities and do not use it internally at all. Instead they tie a leaf around a patient's arm to relieve pain.

Literature. Again it is most annoying that Haskins does not give the source of his information. It is mentioned that the hellebore is considered potent medicine and that a bit of the root chewed and spit on the water causes sea monsters to disappear; but at the end of the paragraph, the root is called drastic poison.[137]

Gathercoal and Wirth say that the medicinal value of *Veratrum viride* was known to the Indians of the eastern and central United States, and that they introduced it to the whites.[138] Youngken states that the roots and rhizomes are used as a cathartic, respiratory, vasculatory, and motor depressant, also to slow overactive heart, reduce blood pressure; it is always used in small dosage.[139]

Allium cernuum Roth. Nodding Onion.

Klallam	q!oxwoi'etc
Makah	klī''yĕ'klī'yĕbupt

Food. Onions are eaten sparingly by the Makah, usually only when traveling alone, their reaction being much like ours today. They are not plentiful enough to be eaten in large quantity. The Klallam and Quinault also eat them.

Medicine. The Makah chew the plant and put it on the chest for pleurisy pains. The Quinault, who found the wild onion only at Lake Quinault, use it the same way.

Literature. Various species of *Allium* are listed in Youngken as diuretics and expectorants.[140] Menzies recorded in his Journal that he saw wild onion with *Arenaria* on Cypress Island on June 8, 1792, and four days later he landed at Birch Bay where he noted a "new species of allium, 6-10 inches high with pink flowers," a good description of the local variety.[141]

Haskins states, "All species of wild onions are known and used as food by the Indians of the Pacific Coast."[142] It is mentioned in the Journals of Lewis and Clark as an article of food and commerce. It is mentioned as a remedy for flatulence due to eating too much camas, and it is used as a poultice.

Brodiaea pulchella (Salisb.) Greene.

This plant was found only once when it could be shown to an informant. The Squaxin informant who saw it did not recognize it.

Camassia Quamash (Pursh) Greene. (*Quamasia azurea* Heller; *Q. quamash* (Pursh) Coville.) Camas.

Chehalis	x̣ka'um; sqaᴇ'q, cooked bulb
Cowlitz	wak'amo
Klallam	kɬoi
Lummi	(LaCamas)
Makah	kwa'dis
Nisqually	sx̣a'dabs
Puyallup	sxɑ'dsɑm[143]
Quileute	k'wala
Quinault	kĕlek
Skokomish	k!a'awūp
Squaxin	sxa'dzaĕb

Food. While the tribes listed above identified specimens of camas, it is universally used in the area, and traded from others if it is not available in the home territory. Except for choice varieties of dried salmon there was no article of food that was more widely traded than camas. The Lummi informant knew no other name than LaCamas, the name for camas in the Chinook jargon, attributable to the French voyageurs.[144]

The camas grows best in prairies (open spaces in the heavily wooded landscape of this area), and is dug in the late spring. Camas bulbs are usually cooked in a pit in the ground. The Nisqually dry them in the sun after cooking and store them for future use. They also cache them in baskets lined with maple leaves, set up in trees, to be used when traveling. The Chehalis smash the bulbs and press them together like a cheese to preserve them. These are boiled in a stew with salmon. The Quileute get camas on Quillayute Prairie and Forks Prairie and prefer to take them after the blossoms have faded. The Quinault find camas at Baker's Prairie, Cook and O'Toole prairies. The Lummi find the best bulbs in May on Matia, Barnes, Spieden, and Clark islands. The Skokomish get camas from the vicinity of Chehalis through trade, since the plant does not grow in their own lands.

Literature. Reagan describes the method of preparing camas by the Quileute. He speaks of oven mounds scattered throughout the region and northward to the Fraser River Country. To substantiate this statement would require further study.[145]

[136] Muenscher, p. 43.
[137] Haskins, p. 49.
[138] Gathercoal and Wirth, p. 133.
[139] Youngken, p. 142.
[140] *Ibid.*, p. 149.
[141] Menzies, pp. 51, 54.

[142] Haskins, p. 15.
[143] Smith, p. 251.
[144] Swan, *Northwest Coast*, pp. 90, 91.
[145] Reagan, p. 60.

Erythronium oregonum Applegate. Fawn Lily.

On the Swinomish Reservation a specimen was shown to three people, all of whom knew where it grew, but could not name it. The Quinault informant, who likewise had no name for it, said it grew around Skokomish, but not at Taholah.

Lilium columbianum Hans. (*L. parviflorum* (Hook.) Holz.) Tiger Lily.[146]

Makah	i'kūp
Puyallup	sa'gwɪtc[147]
Quileute	lilīpewa'de'yu (put)
Quinault	k'laka', "to slash it down"
Skagit	tsa'gwitc
Skokomish	basīltci
Snohomish	tsa'gwitc
Swinomish	tsa'gwitc

Food. Wherever this lily is used, the corm or "bulb" is steamed and eaten. It is gathered by the Klallam in the late fall and buried in a hole lined with cedar boughs to keep fresh. This hole is dug in the house. The Quileute and Quinault gather these lilies where they get camas. The Skagit gather some while they are blooming; if they do not want to dig all the bulbs, stakes are set out around the place where many lilies are growing so that the bulbs can be found when the blossoms are gone and the foliage is dead. The Skagit go to burnt-over land near Birdsview for these lilies. After digging the bulbs, they dig the leaves under to help the next crop, the only semblance of agricultural procedure found in this region. The Samish, closely associated with the Lower Skagit, go to German Prairie, north of Burlington, for their lilies. The Swinomish dig them near Coupeville on Whidbey Island. The Lummi have to leave the present reservation and go to some small islands beyond Lummi Island for them. The Skokomish dig the bulbs just after the lily blooms. It grows profusely in their country.

Literature. Haskins says they are edible and highly prized by coast Indians.[148]

Clintonia uniflora (Schult.) Kunth. One-flowered Clintonia.

Cowlitz	hwik'hwakuɫ

Medicine. The plant is smashed and the juice applied to a cut or to the eyes if they are sore and the lids stick together on awakening.

Streptopus amplexifolius (L.) DC. Twisted-stalk.

Quileute	ya'i'wa'put, "snake plant" (ya"i'wa, snake)

Beliefs. The berries are believed by the Quileute to be eaten by garter snakes and water snakes.

Medicine. The Makah chew and swallow the roots to produce labor in case of protracted delay. An expectant mother would spot some of the plant so she could find it easily if needed.[149]

Disporum Smithii (Hook.) Piper. Bellwort.

This variety was found only in Makah territory, where it is used as a love medicine, but the informant claimed not to know the exact procedure.

Disporum oreganum (Wats.) Benth. & Hook. Fairy Bells.

Skagit	spats (Upper Skagit, sɛtcet'wats, sqwalā'xlad)

As can be seen from the meager list and even more meager naming, this plant is not important. Even the Skagit, who have a name for it, do not use it. The Lummi call them snake berries and warn against touching them. The Klallam say the berries are poisonous and make one very sick. The Swinomish informant did not know the plant. The Makah use some part of the plant as a love medicine, but the informant did not know the procedure.

Maianthemum dilatatum (Wood) Nels. & Macbr. (*Unifolium bifolium kamtschaticum* (Gmel.) Piper.) Wild Lily-of-the-valley; Snakeberry.

Klallam	kɫě'a'tcais
Lummi	x̣'x̣ko'n'č
Makah	tli'ikibupt, "snake plant"
Quileute	tse'a'tsiɫput, "kind of sour"[150]
Quinault	kɫě'qwan

Food. Wherever the plant is used, the berries are eaten but not greatly relished. The Lummi informant says they were not well known. The Quileute say the berries are very oily and in their name for them compare them to whale oil. The Skagit informant did not recognize the plant.

Medicine. The Makah chew the long roots and swallow the juice to correct sterility. The Quinault pound the roots and soak them in water, which they rub on the eyes for soreness.

Literature. Haskins states that the berries were used as food by the Indians from Vancouver Island to Alaska, though they were not always plentiful enough to be of great importance in this district.[151] The pharmacognosies do not substantiate the medicinal purposes cited above.

Trillium ovatum Pursh. Trillium.

Lummi	tcelta'les
Makah	tcatca'olk!us, "sad flower"
Quileute	kokots'tada'ktcɫ, "thieves' leaves"
Skagit	x!at't!ek'ᵘ
Snohomish	tcū'xtcob (generic word for flower)

[146] Jones gives only lily as the common name, but the local people all refer to it as the tiger lily.
[147] Smith, p. 251.
[148] Haskins, p. 21.
[149] Densmore, p. 317.
[150] Another translation by another informant is "t'sea', whale oil."
[151] Haskins, p. 53.

Medicine. Both the Lummi and Skagit use trillium for the eyes, the former dropping the juice of the bulb in the eye for soreness, the latter soaking the roots in water which is then used as an eye wash. The other Skagit informant, however, said the plant was a kind of poison and not used. The Quileute scrape the bulb with a sharp rock and smear this on a boil to bring it to a head.

Charms. The Makah pound the bulb and rub it on the body as a love medicine. The Quinault also attribute this power to the plant, for a woman will cook the bulb and drop it in the food of a man she wants as a lover. Among the Quinault the old people stop children from picking this plant, because such an act brings rain.

The Swinomish informant said she had never seen the plant. The specimen shown her had no blossom, so perhaps the lack of recognition might be understood. The Snohomish had no special name or use for the plant.

Literature. Like Haskins, Stuhr does not mention Indians by tribes, but states that trillium was used as an emetic and for female disorders.[152] The latter is interesting, since there is a statement in Youngken that some species of trillium are recognized as emmenagogues.[153]

ORCHIDACEAE. Orchid Family

Peramium decipiens (Hook.) Piper. Rattlesnake Plantain.

| Cowlitz | mli'smli's |
| Klallam | swuxkla"ants |

Medicine and charms. This plant is not easy to find and so was seldom shown to an informant. The Cowlitz make it into a tea which is used as a tonic. The Klallam informant, who is a devout Shaker, said that since she is a Christian she should not think of such matters, but formerly women rubbed this plant on their bodies to make their husbands like them better.

SALICACEAE. Willow Family

The identification of the willow is difficult and often the specimens brought were not of the best. It is also a problem to know whether the identification of informants was for the particular willow presented to them. It is strange that the commonest willow of the Olympic Peninsula, *S. Scouleriana*, for instance, never appeared.

Populus trichocarpa T. & G. Cottonwood.

Chehalis	nE·'k'wɫ
Cowlitz	xu'pxp
Green River	q'ʷde"q'ats[154]
Quinault	kalle'tsaɫx
Squaxin	stsa'pats

Materials. The Quinault use cottonwood for posts in palisades around villages,[155] and the bark is used by shiftless people for house coverings. For the hearth board of the fire drill, the Cowlitz use cottonwood. The Squaxin use young shoots of cottonwood for making the sweat lodge, and also use them for lashings and tying thongs.

Medicine. The bark is boiled by the Squaxin and the infusion used for a gargle to cure a sore throat. They also bruise the leaves and put them in water to use as an antiseptic on cuts. The Klallam, according to Eells,[156] use the buds for preparing an eye wash. The Quinault, perhaps recognizing the same antiseptic quality the Squaxin believe the plant possesses, use the gum of the burls directly on cuts and wounds and also use the bark at the surface of the ground to make an infusion for the relief of tuberculosis.[155]

Beliefs. The old people, according to a Chehalis informant, used to say that this tree had a life of its own, because it shook itself when there was no wind. Consequently they did not even use it as firewood.

Literature. Another variety of cottonwood, *Populus balsamifera*, is used medicinally, according to Youngken, as a stimulant and an expectorant, the buds and bark being reduced to charcoal.[157]

Salix sp. Willow.

The Klallam call all willows sqwe'e'eltc and regard them as principally useful for the bark, which is made into string. The bark is also boiled as a remedy for sore throat and tuberculosis.

Salix lasiandra Benth. (*Salix lasiandra Lyallii* Sarg.)

| Chehalis | qa'litnts |
| Cowlitz | duxsha'u |

Materials. The Chehalis take the inner bark from the larger trees and twist a two-ply string. The Cowlitz use this wood for the drill of the fire drill.

Salix Piperi Bebb

| Quileute | lila'k'a, "willow" |

Materials. This tree is used extensively by the Quileute, the bark being used in basketry, and the young trees about three or four inches thick being cut for fish weir poles because willows will take root wherever planted. A few leaves of this willow are put in the cooking basket to give the food a good flavor.

Medicine. The roots are used by an athlete in training, to rub his body.

Salix sitchensis Sanson

| Klallam | sqwe'ɛ'eltc |
| Skagit | tsox'alo'ats |

Materials. The Klallam peel the bark and twist it for string.

---

[152] Stuhr, p. 48.
[153] Youngken, p. 169.
[154] Ballard.

[155] Olson, pp. 117, 65, 180, 181.
[156] Eells, pp. 618, 623.
[157] Youngken, p. 121.

Medicine. The bark is peeled and boiled for a tonic.

Miscellaneous. This willow is considered good beaver food. The specimen shown this informant had a gall on it, of which she said, "That berry is the worm's house." The Klallam use the same name for all willows.

Salix Hookeriana Barratt

Makah kl̥k'tci'bupt, "dog plant"

Materials. The Lummi use the bark of saplings, made into string, for duck nets and for reef nets.[158] The Snohomish also make a two-ply string of the bark. The Quinault, using the bark, make a heavier line for tumplines and slings, and give it its most severe test as the harpoon line in sea-lion hunting gear. The Quinault also use the wood as a fish lure or plug for halibut, sole, cod, and flounder.[159]

Medicine. The Makah use the leaves of this willow as an antidote for shell-fish poisoning. They also soak the roots and use the water as a hair wash.

BETULACEAE. Birch Family

Corylus californica (A. DC.) Rose. Hazelnut.

In open woods, common.

Chehalis	k'ap'u'x̣wunl̥, whole plant; k'ap'u'x̣, nut
Cowlitz	k'ko'sas, whole tree; yuka'yuka', catkin
Lummi	kl̥op'uxĕlc
Skagit	k'apox'
Skokomish	k'apūxwai, "nut bush"
Snohomish	kl̥apō'xwats
Squaxin	qaBu'x̣wats, whole plant; qa'Bux, nuts
Swinomish	k'apō'x·

Food. The Cowlitz bury the nuts for winter in a cylindrical type of fish trap. The Chehalis and Puyallup[160] eat the nuts fresh and also store them for winter. The Squaxin bury the nuts in a dry place wrapped in hazel leaves. The Skagit eat the nuts fresh and crack them with a stone; they never store them. The Lummi, Snohomish, and Swinomish also eat them fresh.

Materials. The Chehalis use the twigs twisted to tie things, but they do not make rope of them. The Skokomish use the long twigs for rope, made by twisting.

Literature. In Menzies, *Journal of Vancouver's Voyage,* there is a record of *Corylus californica* at Hannon Point, May 10, 1792.[161]

Alnus oregona Nutt. Alder.

Klallam	s'ko'niltc
Quinault	mal̥p
Swinomish	su·k'uba'ts

Food. The food value of the alder is apparently of no great importance. Only one instance is recorded of the eating of any part of the alder and that is the use of the sap by the Swinomish, who take it from the inside of the bark only when the tide is coming in.

Material. The wood of the alder is, next to cedar, the most widely used in Northwest Coast woodworking. Dishes, spoons, and platters are made of it, but the Swinomish regard it as too soft for canoe paddles. The Quinault make the fire drill and canoe bailer of alder[162] and do not scorn it for canoe paddles. The Quileute even regard alder as superior for paddles because if it is cut green and seasoned it will not split in the hot sun. The Makah make the baby's cradle of alder. Uniformly in this area alder wood is preferred for smoking salmon. It is also used for firewood in the open because it does not spark.

The bark of the alder is used for dye by the Quinault, Snohomish, Lummi, and Quileute. The dye is especially useful to make fish nets invisible to fish. It is also widely used on cedar bark. Its color is described as from red to brown. The bark is also used by the Quinault and Swinomish to line the pot in which elderberries are stored.

The Nisqually use the boughs as covering for temporary shelters.[163]

Medicine. The bark is boiled by the Swinomish and the tea drunk for colds, stomach trouble, and scrofula sores. The Cowlitz rub the rotten wood on the body to ease "aching bones." The Quileute eat the cones raw to stop dysentery and the Klallam chew the catkins as a cure for diarrhoea.

Literature. Reagan mentions the extensive use of alder including the choice of alder trees by the Quileute as the place to put the canoes containing corpses.[164] Menzies has several entries of alder in his Journal,[165] and Swan speaks of the use of "black alder" bark for dyeing basketry grasses.[166] Stuhr lists the use of bark, twigs, and buds as tonics and teas and also mentions an ointment of bark to cure eruptive skin diseases.[167]

FAGACEAE. Beech Family

Quercus Garryana Dougl. Oak.

The oak occurs in this area only where there is open prairie country.

Chehalis	sk'wi'sl̥; skɛkslal̥ox, little oak; kl̥loi, little leaves
Cowlitz	ts'u'nips
Klallam	ql̥apūt
Squaxin	tca'dzats

Food. The Nisqually, Chehalis, Cowlitz, and Squaxin, who live in sections where oak trees are most numerous, use the acorn as food, but in the true

[158] Stern, pp. 41, 43.
[159] Olson, pp. 36, 48, 77, 88.
[160] Smith, p. 252.
[161] Menzies, p. 27.
[162] Olson, pp. 77, 72.
[163] Haeberlin and Gunther, p. 18.
[164] Reagan, p. 61.
[165] Menzies, pp. 20, 49.
[166] Swan, *Northwest Coast,* p. 163.
[167] Stuhr, p. 21.

evergreen forest area that is an unknown dish. The Chehalis roast acorns in the fire. Acorns are stored in baskets of young maple bark and buried in the mud of a slough all winter. In the spring when they are taken out to eat, they look as though they were spoilt, but they are delicious. The Cowlitz bury acorns in the mud to leach them. The Squaxin roast them on hot rocks. The Klallam eat the acorn as a nut without any preparation.[168] The Quinault never use them as food. Since they are eaten in such small quantities the amount of tannic acid in them is not dangerous, and the elaborate leaching process used in northwest California, where the acorn is a basic food, is not necessary.

Materials. The Cowlitz use the wood for making digging sticks and combs, and also as fuel. The Chehalis and others mentioned do not use the wood.

Medicine. The Cowlitz boil the bark as a cure for tuberculosis.

Literature. The presence of the oak in this region was noted by Menzies, who was at Oak Cove near Port Ludlow on May 9, 1792.[169]

URTICACEAE. Nettle Family

Urtica Lyallii Wats. Nettle.

Chehalis	qwunqwu'n, "it stings you"
Cowlitz	ala'la
Klallam	ts!tcexalts
Lummi	tsɪ'ts'tcaɫ
Makah	kalū'p'ki
Quileute	padakokoxɫ, "it blisters"
Quinault	qwunɛn
Samish	tsitsxa'ɪtc
Skagit	tsud'sk!
Skokomish	kɫɑ'ū"kwai
Snohomish	tsudts'x
Squaxin	stu'd'x̣
Swinomish	su'tsx̣, "it'll sting you"

Materials. In almost this entire area the bark of the nettle is peeled, dried, and rolled on the thigh into a two-ply string. The Skagit informant had heard of this string, but had never seen any. The Cowlitz informant said that this type of twine was not used by them. It may be that the cord made of Indian hemp was secured by the Cowlitz from eastern Washington. A description of the making of this string by the Lummi is given by Stern.[170] This string is used for duck nets by the Lummi, Snohomish, and Skokomish.

Medicine. The medicinal value of this plant seems to be as great as its power of irritation. The Chehalis and Quileute take the whole stalk and whip a person having rheumatism, while the Quinault count that as a help for paralysis. For the same illness, the Cowlitz crush the sprout and use it as a poultice.

Rubbing with nettles is also good for colds, according to the Snohomish. Perhaps less drastic and also less specific, baths are taken by the Samish and Swinomish in an infusion made of the entire nettle plant and the white fir (*Abies grandis*), pounded together and boiled. It serves as a general tonic. The Skagit do the same for colds. The roots are boiled to make a hair wash especially for girls by the Chehalis and Skokomish. The Klallam soak the stalk in water and rub the body with it, for soreness or stiffness. Internally, infusions of nettles are used for some of the same ailments. The Quileute pound the root and drink the boiled infusion for rheumatism, a small Chinese teacup full being the dosage. This is one of the few occasions when a dosage was given. The Squaxin crush the leaves and put them in water as a drink for a woman having difficulties in childbirth. This "scares the baby out," for the nettles are after him, according to the informant. The Lummi also drink nettles during childbirth.[171] Believing that a tea made of nettles would relax the muscles, the Cowlitz give it to a woman about to deliver a child. The Snohomish drink the same infusion for colds. The Quinault peel the bark and boil that as a cure for headache and nosebleed. They also give the tips of the plant to a woman to chew during labor.

Charms. The Makah rub the body with nettles after handling a corpse, as a matter of purification. The Quileute seal hunter rubs himself with nettles before going out, to help him stay awake through the night.

Literature. The nettle is one of the most common plants in western Washington, proving especially annoying in the underbrush. Reagan[172] says that where the Quileute women clear the nettles away they make their best gardens. He mentions the use of nettles as food and so does Haskins,[173] but nowhere in this study was that use brought forth. Menzies saw nettles at Birch Bay.[174] Swan states that a yellow dye is made of nettle roots mixed with a shrub traded from northern Indians.[175] Stuhr indicates the modern pharmaceutical use of nettles as a counter-irritant and alterative.[176]

ARISTOLOCHIACEAE. Birthwort Family

Asarum caudatum Lindl. Wild Ginger.

Green River	xwaltcl[177]
Skagit	tuxop'bida'libut; tuxop', "pheasant;" (because pheasants eat it) (Mrs. Moses)
	qwolqwalted (Mr. Moses)
Upper Skagit	tceltceltcalaqwe'tc

[168] Gunther, p. 198.
[169] Menzies, p. 26.
[170] Stern, p. 63.

[171] Stern, p. 14.
[172] Reagan, p. 61.
[173] Haskins, p. 77.
[174] Menzies, p. 53.
[175] Swan, *Northwest Coast*, p. 163.
[176] Stuhr, No. 139.
[177] Ballard.

Medicine. The Skagit are the only tribe from which a definite use was obtained for this plant. The leaves are dried with another plant and used for tuberculosis. Eating the leaves gives one appetite. The Upper Skagit boil it as a tonic tea.

The Lummi informant saw a specimen, but did not recognize it.

POLYGONACEAE. Buckwheat Family

Rumex sp. Dock.

Chehalis	k'alemat(xʔ)unɬ
Cowlitz	te'lwa'cus

Food. The Chehalis cook the green stalks of the larger plants over maple and cedar limbs on hot rocks.

Medicine. The Cowlitz boil the stalk and use the water as an antiseptic wash for leg sores.

Rumex Acetosella L. Sheep-sorrel Dock.

Chehalis	tc'ayu'ẋu, "sour leaves"

Food. The leaves are eaten raw or boiled by the Chehalis.

Medicine. The Squaxin eat the leaves raw to cure tuberculosis. The informant, however, could not recall the name of the plant.

Literature. Stuhr indicates that the root is astringent and the leaves acrid and refrigerant.[178]

Rumex obtusifolius L. Bitter Dock.

Charm. The Quinault women believe that if the leaves of this dock are burned with soiled sanitary napkins, the menstrual flow will stop.[179]

NYCTAGINACEAE. Four-o'clock Family

Abronia latifolia Esch. Sand Verbena.

Food. The large roots are eaten by both Klallam and Makah. The Klallam informant compared them to sugar beets. The Makah eat them in the fall.

Literature. Both Haskins and Stuhr mention the Indian use of the roots as food.[180]

PORTULACACEAE. Purslane Family

Claytonia sibirica L. (*Limnia washingtoniana* (Suksd.) Rydb.) Spring Beauty, Miner's Lettuce.

Cowlitz	anipaswa'kuɬ
Quileute	pᴇpᴇ'tcitsep, "red at the ground"
Skagit	skokxᵘ'tca'd
Skykomish	tsak'a'ẋwulqᴇd, "makes the hair grow"
Snohomish	sto'ltū·xked

Medicine. The Quileute make a tea of this plant and drink it as a urinative. They also squeeze the stem with the fingers and rub the juice on the eyes. The Quinault women chew the whole plant during pregnancy so the baby will be soft when born. The Skagit drink a tea made of the plant as a general tonic; one specific example was given where this tea cured a sore throat. The Snohomish, Quileute, Skykomish, and Cowlitz rub the stem between the palms, and rub the plant in cold water which in turn is rubbed on the hair as a tonic. All agree that it makes the hair glossy, and the Quileute believe it prevents dandruff.[181]

The Lummi informants did not recognize it.

Literature. The following entry is from Menzies' Journal: "In this walk I found growing in the crevices of a small rock about midway between two points a new species of Claytonia; as I met with it no where else in my journey, it must be considered as a rare plant in this country." (*Claytonia furcata*, May 7, 1792.)[182]

NYMPHAEACEAE. Water Lily Family

Nymphozanthus polysepalus (Engelm.) Fernald. (*Nymphaea polysepala* (Engelm.) Greene.)

Medicine. No informant could recall the native name of this plant which everywhere is used medicinally. The Makah steam a patient over the roots. The Quinault heat the roots and apply them to the seat of the pain, especially for rheumatism. They go two and one-half miles up river for these lilies. The Quinault believe that some roots look like men and some like women, so they always pick one appropriate to the patient.

RANUNCULACEAE. Buttercup Family[183]

Anemone sp.

Cowlitz	lu'la'
Quileute	t'a'o'·l[184]

Medicine. A specimen of this was recognized oɴly by the Cowlitz informant who stated that a tea is made of it and drunk for tuberculosis. The dose should be small, because too much would burn the stomach.

Ranunculus reptans L. (*R. Flammula* L., var. *reptans* (L.) Schlecht.) Buttercup.

Makah	kɬītc'sapbupt, whole plant; kɬitc'sap, leaves
Quileute	t'a'o'·l[185]

[178] Stuhr, No. 107.

[179] Found by Densmore among the Makah, who call it hua'psi, meaning "breaks up a plan." "This medicine was used when a person was conscious of being near an enemy which meant death. The fresh roots were pounded and rubbed on the body. A man would pay from five to ten blankets for one application of this remedy. When 'given out' this and similar plants were pounded and fixed so they could not be recognized." Densmore, p. 321.

[180] Haskins, p. 85; Stuhr, p. 95.

[181] According to Densmore, p. 314, the Makah pound this plant and apply it to the abdomen as a remedy for constipation.

[182] Menzies, p. 23.

[183] A buttercup (*Ranunculus* sp.) was used by the Makah as a poultice. The mashed leaves, used sparingly—for they themselves would make a sore—were applied to open and heal sore glands. Densmore, p. 315. *Ranunculus bongardi* Greene was also used as a poultice by the Makah to prevent blood poisoning. The poultice was covered with a small shell. Densmore, p. 316.

[184] Andrade, p. 164. This word was found in Andrade's vocabulary, but no use was given.

[185] Andrade, p. 164.

Food. The roots of the plant are dug between September and February and cooked on hot rocks. The roots are dipped in whale or seal oil and eaten with dried salmon eggs.

The Snohomish informant recognized it as a local wild flower, but had no name for it.

Ranunculus sp. Buttercup.

The Skokomish call this plant tsĭbolk!o'obic and eat the roots as winter food.

Delphinium Menziesii DC. (*D. columbianum* ex p. of Piper, not Nutt.) Larkspur.

Chehalis	k'a'x̣k'anĭ; k'a'x̣, "rub it around"
Green River	tcitcila'xwa'ts (diminutive of tcila^x, "quiver")

Medicine. The Chehalis put the stalks and roots in warm ashes and use them for poultices. This is good for sores. The whole plant is poisonous and needs to be handled by someone who understands its use. The informant added that it is poisonous to eat.[186]

It is not known to the Squaxin.

Literature. Another species (*D. Ajacis*) is known as a parisiticide; it is also given internally as a cardiac stimulant.[187]

Aquilegia formosa Fisch. Columbine.

Chehalis	ya'ri'siyans, "it's good on your teeth"
Cowlitz	t'u'mts
Green River	tsu'dbsmus *or* tsumsamus[188]
Quileute	k'lĭ'lixlix, "to make a scar" *or* pě'ĭtcabixa'a, "red flowers"

Medicine. The Quileute scrape the roots with a sharp rock and smear the milky pulp on sores to help form a scar. The leaves are also chewed and spit on sores.

Miscellaneous. The Chehalis children suck the honey out of the flowers.

The Cowlitz have a name for it but no use. The Squaxin do not know it, nor do the Skagit. The Quinault informant had seen the plant, but knows no name for it. Although it grows plentifully at Hobuck, the Makah have no name or use for it.

Actaea arguta Nutt. (*A. asplenifolia* Greene.) Baneberry.

Quileute	koloqwixɬ, "open the place"
Quinault	pa'masɬm, "cold"
Snohomish	tcetwudsko'lasad

Medicine. The Quileute chew the leaves and spit them on a boil to bring it to a head. The Quinault did the same for wounds received in old time fighting. Later it has been used on gunshot wounds.

Beliefs. The Snohomish believe that bears eat the berries.

BERBERIDACEAE. Barberry Family

Berberis sp. Oregon Grape.

In some instances, especially in references taken from the literature, *Berberis* was not separated into the two varieties, so these instances are discussed here.

Chehalis	kiohwizlnĭ
Cowlitz	(ĭ)k'wa'ukawus
Lummi	sunnĭ'
Makah	kluksitɬkobupt, "raven plant"

Food. The Cowlitz eat the berries raw or boiled, but never dry them for preserving. The Makah regard the berries only as raven food and say they make children ill. The Lummi eat the berries, as do the Lower Chinook.[189]

Materials. The Chehalis use the unidentified *Berberis* in the same manner as the *Berberis Aquifolium*, namely, the roots are boiled for dye.[190] The Makah, who do not find Oregon grape in their own territory, use the root for dye; they trade for it or gather it when traveling. The same is true of the Quinault,[191] who do not find it near Taholah, but near Lake Quinault. The Cowlitz also make dye of the root. The Lummi, according to one informant, do not know of the dye, but another knew of its use.

Medicine. The root is boiled and the liquid drunk to cure coughs and stomach disorders, by the Quinault.[192] The Cowlitz boil the bark and use the infusion to wash sores on the skin and in the mouth.

Berberis Aquifolium Pursh. Oregon Grape (tall bush).

Chehalis	tc'iyu'xwitsnĭ
Samish	xwe·sbɑ'dats
Skagit	tĕko'lqwix
Snohomish	qu'bqubitc
Swinomish	sqwa"tcas

Food. The Samish, Swinomish, and Snohomish eat the fresh berries. The Squaxin eat the berries also, but say they are too dry and sour to be good. The Chehalis do not eat the berries.

Materials. The root of *B. Aquifolium* and *B. nervosa* are used indiscriminately for yellow dye by the Snohomish, Skagit, and Chehalis.

Medicine. The Squaxin prepare a tea of the roots to be used as a gargle for sore throat and drunk in spring to purify the blood. The Skagit use the root for medicine, but the informant could not be specific. The Swinomish and Samish make a tea of the root for a general tonic.

Berberis nervosa. Pursh.

Klallam	cu't'tcin
Snohomish	swaix'ats
Upper Skagit	kōmkomtc, berries; kōmkō'mtcalcid, roots

[186] Listed as such by Muenscher, p. 83.
[187] Youngken, p. 296.
[188] Ballard, who thinks this may be a Sahaptin word.
[189] Ray, p. 123.
[190] Adamson, MS Notes.
[191] Olson, p. 81.
[192] Olson, p. 181.

Food. The Upper Skagit used to eat the ripe berries; now they make jam of them. The specimen discussed was *B. nervosa,* but the informant said that the same name was applied to both kinds and added that white people refer to this plant as wild grape.

Materials. All the groups mentioned above use the roots for dyeing basketry materials, especially *Xerophyllum tenax.* The Upper Skagit informant added that they use the dye now on rags for braided rugs.

Medicine. The Upper Skagit boil the roots and drink the juice for venereal disease.

Literature. Haskins notes the use of Oregon grape for dye and food. Also mentioned is the fact that the white man has learned of the medicinal value of this plant, and tons are dug each year and marketed.[193] Gathercoal and Wirth confirm this statement by the information that commercial supplies come from Washington, Oregon, and California. In our materia medica it is cited as a bitter tonic and alterative.[194] Youngken adds that it is given as a stimulant to appetite—perhaps the same reason for the general tonic use of it by the local Indians.[195]

Achlys triphylla (Smith) DC. Vanilla Leaf.

Lummi	su'ktcen; xɬwɛ'l'ɬos
Skagit	kakada'lɛxid, "crow food"

Medicine. The Cowlitz use the leaves in an infusion drunk for tuberculosis, but the informant knew no name for it. The Skagit also use it for tuberculosis, and they boil the leaves for a hair wash. This use is also known to one Lummi informant. The other Lummi informant said the plant was mashed and soaked in water which was drunk as an emetic.

FUMARIACEAE. Fumitory Family

Dicentra formosa (Andr.) DC. (*Bikukulla formosa* (Andr.) Coville.) Wild Bleeding-heart.

Cowlitz	xwoixwoi'as, name of plant; tumla'-tumla', "little hearts"
Green River	tsatsa'tsu'we[196]
Skagit	cecqwa'lkalɛ, "toothache medicine"
Upper Skagit	t'at'ai'ɛ''bcid xadɛxlidts'o'latc, "medicine for worms" (ts'o'latc, worms)

Medicine. While the Cowlitz recognize the plant, they have no use for it. The Quinault know it grows near Oakville but not at Taholah, and have no name for it. The Green River information consists of the name only. The Upper Skagit, as the name indicates, use it as a worm medicine, the root being pounded and boiled. The other Skagit informant referred to it as toothache medicine and said the roots were chewed to cure toothache. Another Skagit said the plant was crushed and put on the hair, or crushed in water

and the hair washed with it. It is especially good for young children, because it makes the hair grow.

CRASSULACEAE. Stonecrop Family

Sedum sp. Stonecrop.

This plant is known to the Makah as tcatca''klk, water plant, because of its succulent nature. It is eaten when on journeys, if there is any doubt about the safety of the water in the locality. The fear about the water is not due to any knowledge of harmful bacteria, but to a belief in malicious spirits.[197] The Quinault informant did not know the plant.

SAXIFRAGACEAE. Saxifrage Family

Boykinia elata (Nutt.) Greene. (*Therefon elatum* (Nutt.) Greene.)

Quileute	tcɪwawuxtcɛ'ɑxɫa

Medicine. The leaves of this plant are eaten for tuberculosis by the Quileute.

Tiarella trifoliata L.

Quileute	qwaqwlatcyu'ɫ, "three leaves"; (qwa''ɫ, three)

Medicine. The Quileute chew the leaves as a cough medicine.

Tellima grandiflora (Pursh) Dougl. Fringe-cup.

Skagit	t'axōbdaloxid

Medicine. The Skagit pound the whole plant, boil it and drink the tea for any kind of sickness. It especially restores appetite.

Heuchera micrantha Dougl. (*H. diversifolia* Rydb.) Alumroot.

The Skagit informant could not recall the name for this plant, but knew that it is pounded and rubbed on the hair of little girls to make it grow thick. It is also put on cuts.

Stuhr lists the plant as being an astringent.[198]

Tolmiea Menziesii (Pursh) T. & G. (*Leptaxis Menziesii* (Pursh) Raf.) Youth-on-age.

Cowlitz	t'satsu'ms spama' tautmi'kʷ, "medicine for boils"
Makah	tca'c'wɛ

Food. The Makah eat the sprouts raw in the early spring.

Medicine. The leaf is applied fresh to a boil by the Cowlitz.

Philadelphus Gordonianus Lindl. Mock-orange (Syringa).

Cowlitz	sa'xit
Lummi	tsitsinalitc *or* tsɛtsɛ'tc
Skagit	ts'o'latatc
Snohomish	tsulota'tci'ats *or* tsaigɑ'sɪdats

[193] Haskins, p. 118.
[194] Gathercoal and Wirth, pp. 270, 271.
[195] Youngken, p. 303.
[196] Ballard.

[197] According to Densmore called cha'chakli, "filled with water," and chewed by Makah women to bring on menstrual periods. Densmore, p. 317.
[198] Stuhr, p. 126.

Materials. The wood is used for making combs by the Cowlitz and the Lummi, while the Skagit make arrowshafts "and many other things" of it. The Lummi use it for netting shuttles, and in response to a more modern need, knitting needles.

Medicine. Rather as a toilet use, the Cowlitz and Snohomish make soapy lather of the bruised leaves and flowers. This lather the Snohomish also rub on sores.

Literature. Menzies saw Mock-orange at Birch Bay on June 15, 1792.[199] Haskins has the following statement: "Young straight shoots were used for bows, but not valued where yew is found. Dr. Cooper reports in 1853, that the Indians macerated the leaves and used them as a substitute for soap."[200]

Ribes divaricatum Dougl. Common Gooseberry.

Cowlitz	tmuxwas
Klallam	t!amanwexitcɬ
Makah	catctka′bupt
Quinault	kɬeʹeʹmwus, "tied on your nose"
Snohomish	tsa′kab(h)ats (according to Swinomish informant)
Swinomish	t′u′bx̣wats, plant; t′u′bx̣w, berry

Food. The Swinomish eat the berries fresh, but never store them. The Quinault baked them in cakes and dried them like other berries.[201] Another informant added that they are mixed with elderberries and buried with them for preservation. They grow at Chinook Creek and Ayhut, but not near Taholah. The Cowlitz gather the berries while they are still green, and dry and store them for winter use; they are also eaten fresh.

Medicine. The Swinomish boil the roots and drink the infusion for sore throat, tuberculosis, and venereal disease. It is sometimes mixed with the roots of *Ribes sanguineum.* The Makah soak the bark and use the water for an eye wash, while the Klallam rinse the inner bark in water mixed with some human milk and use it for the same purpose. The Cowlitz burn and pulverize the woody stem and rub the charcoal on sores on the neck. The Nisqually use the thorn for tattooing, with charcoal for coloring matter.[202]

Literature. Reagan gives kats-ah as the Quileute name for the six varieties of *Grossulariaceae* he lists, and he says the currants are eaten raw.[203]

The absence of any tribes from this list does not mean that they would not recognize the various *Ribes,* but only that I did not have a specimen at hand. The Skagit and Lummi informants saw *Ribes lacustre* and did not distinguish between it and the gooseberry, but one Swinomish informant did.

[199] Menzies, p. 56.
[200] Haskins, p. 137.
[201] Olson, p. 55.
[202] Haeberlin and Gunther, p. 40.
[203] Reagan, p. 62.

Ribes lacustre (Pers.) Poir. Swamp Currant.

Lummi	kamēltc
Skagit	djax′xō′sats
Snohomish	tsɑ′xosats
Swinomish	stikɬa″alkabats

Medicine. The two Skagit informants, although using different names for the plant, agreed that its bark is peeled off and boiled into a tea which is strained and drunk during childbirth. One informant said, "If one eats two of the berries, it won't hurt to get pricked." The thorns of this bush are apt to cause swellings. The other Skagit informant added that the tea is also used as a wash for sore eyes. The Lummi boil the twigs and drink the tea for general body aches. The Snohomish have no use for the plant. The Swinomish informant said that the specimen she was shown was not the "real" one, though known by the same name; and claimed that the thorns of this one were poisonous.

Ribes bracteosum Dougl. Skunk Currant, Wild Currant.

Green River	tsuxtsɑ′la′ts
Makah	k!lōlō″o
Quileute	klo·″o

Food. The Makah eat the berries fresh,[204] as do the Quileute.

Materials. The Quileute remove the pith from the stem and use it as a tube to inflate seal paunches which are used as oil containers. The large leaves are also used by them to line and cover hemlock bark containers in which elderberries are stored.

Medicine. The Green River people make a medicine of the bark taken from the east side of the tree, but Mr. Ballard's informant did not know its specific use.

Ribes laxiflorum Pursh. Trailing Currant.

Green River	po′q *or* po′qwa′ts[205]
Lummi	sko′lɛ′is
Skagit	xalai′tɛt, paiya′kad
Skokomish	p′ūkē
Swinomish	cūcū′k!ᵘ

Food. The Makah eat the berries fresh as do the Skagit and Lummi. No currants were eaten by the Quinault.

Medicine. The Skagit peel the bark and boil it for cold medicine. The Lummi boil both leaves and twigs with another medicine not known to the informant for a general tonic. The Skokomish boil the bark and roots for a tea for tuberculosis. The Swinomish informant knew no use for it, nor is one given for the Green River.

Ribes sanguineum Pursh. Red-flowering Currant.

| Klallam | xuwiˣᵘq!a |

Food. The Klallam eat the berries fresh.[206]

[204] Densmore, p. 320.
[205] Ballard.
[206] Gunther, pp. 197, 206.

ROSACEAE. Rose Family

The rose family is well represented in western Washington and is widely used by the Indians. A general characteristic of the rose family is the presence of tannin, and usually the plant is used for the astringent quality of the tannin, according to Youngken.[207]

Physocarpus capitatus (Pursh) Kuntze. (*Opulaster opulifolius* of Piper Fl. Wash.) Ninebark.

Chehalis	su'k'nł
Green River	"redwood," because it has red young shoots. (Indian word not known.)[208]
Squaxin	pu'qwats, whole plant; pu·'qwa, berry

Medicine. The Green River people use the young shoots, peeled of bark, as an emetic.

Miscellaneous. The Chehalis do not use it, nor do the Squaxin, although they say that children and bears eat the berries.

Holodiscus discolor (Pursh) Maxim. (*Schizonotus discolor* (Pursh) Raf.) Ocean Spray, Spirea.

Chehalis	sqa'tł
Klallam	k!atsi'ltc
Lummi	k'aitsatcł
Makah	tsik'wip
Skagit	katsa'qwats
Snohomish	qatsa'gwats
Squaxin	qatsa'gwats
Swinomish	qatsa'gwats

Material. Colloquially known in English as ironwood, this wood is used for many tools and utensils in this entire region. Every group listed makes roasting tongs of ironwood. The Swinomish informant commented, "Because it won't burn." The Lummi use sticks of ironwood in the first salmon ceremony, breaking them up afterward and throwing them in the river as symbolic of breaking up canoes to show that the salmon intends to stay.[209] Digging sticks, both for clams and roots, are always made of this wood. The prongs of duck spears of the Lummi and Swinomish, as well as the Swinomish flounder spear used in the slough in December and January, are of this wood. The Squaxin add canoe paddles to the many useful articles made of ironwood, and all informants mention shafts, as well as the prongs of spears.

Medicine. The Makah peel the bark and boil it as tea tonic for convalescents and athletes. The Lummi strip the blossoms as a cure for diarrhoea, and soak the inner bark as an eye wash. They also put the leaves on sore lips and feet. The Chehalis boil dried-up bunches of seeds and drink the infusion to stop smallpox, black measles, chicken pox, or any similar

contagious disease. Their near neighbors, the Squaxin, take these same seeds, mix them with wild cherry, and make a blood purifier.

Literature. Haskins mentions only the use of this wood for arrowshafts.[210]

Spiraea Menziesii Hook. Spirea.

Chehalis	sa"nł
Nisqually	stci'lats
Quinault	tsapa'snixł, "it tangles you when you get them"

Materials. The Quinault peel the stems and use them to string clams for roasting. The other tribes mentioned, as well as the Squaxin, have names for the plant, but no special use.

Spiraea Douglasii Hook. Spirea or Hardhack.

Green River	tcītcī'a"lats
Lummi	tĕtclp
Snohomish	tcĕtcēla'ts

The Green River and Snohomish have only a name, but no use for the plant; the Skokomish have no name and no use for it.

Material. The Lummi use this variety of spirea just like *Holodiscus discolor*, principally for spreading and cooking salmon.

Medicine. The Lummi also use the seeds of this variety of spirea as a tea for diarrhoea.

Aruncus sylvester Kostel. (*A. acuminatus* Rydb.; *A. Aruncus* (L.) Karst.) Goat's-beard.

Lummi	pĕstĕdats
Makah	xa'xa'tsbūkkūk, "flowers that look like herring eggs"[211]
Quileute	kłĕlĕ'lixput, whole plant; kłĕlĕ'lix, root
Quinault	pama'slin, "to make you cool"
Skagit	pĕsdĕ'da'ts, "swollen part goes down"

Medicine. The simplest form of goat's-beard as a remedy is used by the Lummi, who chew the leaves to help cure smallpox. Its efficacy on sores is recognized by several groups. The Skagit burn the twigs and mix the ashes with bear grease and put it on swellings, especially on the throat. The roots may be used in the same way. The Klallam, who could not recall the name of the plant, treat the roots in the same way and put the salve on sores that won't heal. The Quileute scrape the root on a sharp rock and smear the pulp on sores. They also pound and boil the root and drink the infusion as a general tonic. The Quileute informant stated that his people got this remedy from the people on Vancouver Island, probably meaning the Nootka, for they have most direct contact with the Quileute through the Makah. Returning to the uses of goat's-beard by the Skagit,

[207] Youngken, p. 363.
[208] Ballard.
[209] Stern, p. 45.

[210] Haskins, p. 167.
[211] hihi'iboklosis, "plant with flowers that look like herring eggs," Densmore, p. 310.

one finds that they also use the roots for an infusion which is drunk as a cure for colds and sore throat. The Makah drink a similar infusion for kidney trouble and gonorrhea.[212]

Literature. This plant is not listed in any pharmacopeia which was consulted.

Rosa Sp.

There are several varieties of roses found in this area, and I was often doubtful, when only one variety could be found, whether the informant gave the species name or one for that variety alone. Twice this question was answered: the Skagit informant said there were several varieties of roses; only the one she was shown (*Rosa nutkana*) was used as she described. The Snohomish informant said of *R. nutkana* that this was the big rose which used to grow profusely in her locality but was hard to find now. *R. gymnocarpa*, found only once, and *R. pisocarpa* were carefully distinguished from *nutkana* by the Snohomish informant. It is, however, noteworthy that this Snohomish informant having both *R. nutkana* and *R. pisocarpa* at hand gave the latter the same name used by the Skagit and Swinomish for *nutkana*. Is that perhaps a general name for rose in that dialect of Salish?

Rosa pisocarpa Gray. Rose.

Chehalis	xwɑle′lamtsɑnł
Snohomish	sk!a′pads

Food. The Squaxin eat the hips fresh. The Chehalis do not eat the hips of any variety of rose. The Snohomish never eat this variety.

Medicine. The Snohomish boil the roots and drink the tea for sore throat. The bark is steeped, and the liquid given by the Squaxin as a soothing drink after childbirth.

Rosa nutkana Presl. Wild Rose.

Chehalis	qɛqaba′wiłat
Cowlitz	tca′pama·c
Lummi	kalakĕ′tc
Makah	k!liqwai″abupt
Quileute	k′ɛq′wai′put
Skagit	sk!a′p!a
Skokomish	yĕyłsta
Snohomish	yĕsta′d
Swinomish	sk!a′p′ats

Food. The Makah eat the rose hips, as do the Klallam, who are more appreciative of them for giving a sweet breath than for food value.[213] The Cowlitz, however, state that only birds eat the hips. The Skagit are fond of combining rose hips with dried salmon eggs. The Swinomish, Snohomish, and Quinault all eat the hips. The Lummi dry them before eating. The Lummi peel the twigs and boil

them as a tea for a beverage. The Skagit make a similar tea of the leaves. The Skokomish eat the rose hips in the fall.

Medicine. The Quinault reduce the twigs to ashes which are mixed with skunk oil and applied to syphilis sores.[214] The Quileute burn the haws and use them in the same way "on swellings." The Skagit boil the roots with sugar and take it by the spoonful as a remedy for sore throat. This sounds like a fairly modern medicine. They also use an infusion of the root as an eye wash. The Cowlitz bathe a baby in water in which the leaves have been boiled, to strengthen him, whether he is ill or well. The bark is boiled into a tea by the Chehalis and given to women in childbirth to ease labor pains.

Literature. Haskins states that on the Pacific coast the rose figures in the folklore as being the last thing people resort to in a period of starvation.[215] If such statements were documented, it would be possible to check them and increase their value. In western Washington no such feeling exists in the minds of any present-day informants. Nor has the rose the sentimental value given it in our culture. It is just another flower, often classed with other thorny plants as being slightly unpleasant.

Rosa gymnocarpa Nutt. Wild Rose.

Only the Chehalis have a name for this rose, "upsaynt", and even they do not use it.

Rubus parviflorus Nutt. Thimbleberry.

Chehalis	k′wa′xwunł, whole plant; k′wa′xʷ, berries
Cowlitz	kᵘku·′cnas
Klallam	łkelitc
Makah	lūlūwa′ts[216]
Quileute	taqa·′tcitlpat; t′aqa·′tcil[217], whole plant; taqa·′tcitł, berries
Quinault	xĕ′ĕ′nis
Samish	t′u′qumi′łtc, whole plant
Snohomish	słaka′ats
Squaxin	słałaqa′ts, whole plant; słała′q, berries
Swinomish	ła′qa′ats
Upper Skagit	sła′ka

Food. The sprouts are eaten in early spring by the Makah, Klallam, Swinomish, Samish, and Upper Skagit. The Samish and Swinomish like to eat them with half-dried salmon eggs. The berries are eaten fresh by the Makah,[218] Cowlitz, Swinomish, Samish, Chehalis, Snohomish, Quileute, Squaxin, Quinault, and Upper Skagit. The Quinault pick the berries unripe and let them stand in baskets. The Squaxin mix the fresh berries with blackberries. Thimble-

---

[212] Densmore lists as the Makah uses of this plant the chewing of the leaves for tuberculosis and the root as a kidney remedy. Densmore, pp. 313, 314.
[213] Makah: the leaves are mashed and used as a poultice for sore eyes or for any severe pain or any form of abscess. Densmore, p. 315. Klallam: Gunther, p. 305.

[214] Olson, p. 181.
[215] Haskins, p. 175.
[216] Lulu′whatsbup, Densmore, p. 311.
[217] Andrade, p. 164; also t′a′qatcil·t′sa, "little thimbleberry," Andrade, p. 165.
[218] Densmore, p. 315.

berries are generally regarded as too soft for drying, but the Squaxin do it nevertheless, and store them in hard or soft baskets.

Materials. The bark is boiled and used as soap by the Cowlitz. The Quileute use the leaves to wrap cooked elderberries for storage. The Quinault use these leaves together with skunk cabbage leaves to line baskets in preserving elderberries.

Medicine. The Makah collect the leaves in the fall, boil them, and drink the tea for anemia and strengthening the blood.[219] The Cowlitz powder the dried leaves and apply them to burns to avoid a scar, while the Upper Skagit burn the leaves and mix the ashes with grease to put on swellings.

Literature. Haskins mentions that the Indians use the young shoots.[220] Reagan says thimbleberries are common everywhere and called tah-ah-chilth or tah-hah-chilth.[221]

There was no reference to thimbleberries in the various pharmacognosies consulted.

This plant is very widely used and has a much wider distribution than is indicated here. In many instances tribes were visited when it was neither in bloom nor in fruit.

Rubus spectabilis Pursh. Salmonberry.

One of the most common shrubs in the fir forests of western Washington.

Chehalis	yɛ′twanł, whole shrub; yɛ′twa, berries	
Cowlitz	e′twanac, whole plant; e′twan, berries	
Green River	kalɛ′tuwa, yellow salmonberry	
Lower Chinook	yunts′[222]	
Lummi	lī′la	
Makah	ka′k'wɛ'abupt[223], plant; ka′k'wɛ, berry	
Quileute	tca'a′xłwap'ut, "It's ripe berries," whole plant; tca'a′xłwa, berries yatc'tsxła, sprouts; tca'a′xłwakło′ŏtcxł, leaves	
Quinault	k'wkłaxnix	
Squaxin	stu′gwaDats, plant; stu′gwaD, berries	
Swinomish	stikwa′dats, plant; stikwa′d, berry; cikwa′'ads, sprouts	

Food. Salmonberries are eaten fresh everywhere and are considered too soft to dry. Sprouts are prepared in a pit in which a fire has been burning. They are eaten with dried salmon. These uses are so universal in this area that it is not necessary to mention specific tribes. Some Indian women today can the salmonberries, under the direction of the Home Economics instructors from the Indian Service.

Materials. More scattered are the other uses of the salmonberry shrub. The Makah dry and peel a branch, remove the pith and use it for a pipe stem.[224] The Quileute plug the hair seal float used in whaling with the hollow stem of elderberry wood and in this hollow stem they insert a piece of salmonberry wood as a stopper. This salmonberry wood plug can be removed for further inflation of the float.

Medicine. An astringent quality must be recognized in the bark and leaves of salmonberry, for the Quileute chew the leaves and spit them on burns, and in winter when leaves are not obtainable they use the bark instead. The Makah pound the bark and lay it on an aching tooth or a festering wound to kill the pain.[225] The Quinault boil the bark in sea water, and the brew is drunk to lessen labor pains. It is also used by them to clean infected wounds, especially burns.

Literature. Reagan gives the words chu-ah-thlus-wah-put, kood, or chu-ah-thlu-wah-put which resemble to a certain degree the Quileute words in the present study. In his discussion he combines all the species of *Rubus*, listing eight varieties.[226] Haskins gives reasons why the plant is called salmonberry by quoting some "Indian" myths, but neglects to mention the tribe or state the source of the information.[227] Swan states that the crisp, astringent quality of the sprouts is a welcome change at a time when people are likely to have overeaten on oily herring. The sprouts are ready for use just at the right time, and continue through the early part of the salmon run, serving the same purpose.[228]

Rubus leucodermis Dougl. Blackcap.

Cowlitz	ca′xatac, bush; ca′xat, berries
Green River	tcɪlkŏbats[229]
Klallam	ts!ko′ma, leaves; sqwamiłtsa'etc, sprouts
Puyallup-Nisqually	tcoko′ba[230]

Food. These berries are probably eaten by more tribes than the few listed above, but like so many other plants were not always available for discussion. The Cowlitz, besides eating them fresh, dry them in the sun or over a fire and store them in a maple-bark basket for winter use. According to Mr. Ballard, the Green River people also dry them. The Klallam eat the sprouts and young leaves, as well as the berries. The Puyallup mix blackcaps with blackberries in drying.

Rubus macropetalus Dougl. (*R. Helleri* Rydb.) Blackberry or Dewberry.

Cowlitz	wisi′kas, bush; wisi′k, berries; wiskalai, "little stickers"

[219] They also powder a growth on this plant and apply it to sores. Densmore, p. 315.
[220] Haskins, p. 172.
[221] Reagan, p. 63.
[222] Name given by Miss Louise Colbert.
[223] kaknip, Densmore, p. 310; kakuip, Densmore, p. 317.

[224] Swan, *Indians of Cape Flattery*, p. 27.
[225] The bark is scraped, chewed, and swallowed to check hemorrhages, following confinement. Densmore, p. 327.
[226] Reagan, p. 63.
[227] Haskins, pp. 173, 174.
[228] Swan, *Northwest Coast*, pp. 87, 88.
[229] Ballard.
[230] Smith, p. 249.

Green River	gwa'dbiɣ[u231]
Lummi	tc'kwanc
Puyallup-Nisqually	gwɑ'dbiaq[u232]
Quileute	bada''abiɣ[w]
Skagit	xukwūda'ts
Snohomish	kūdūbi'xwads, whole plant; kūdū'bix[u], berries

Food. The Quileute, Skagit, and Cowlitz eat the berries both fresh and dried. The Green River people do not mention the drying of the berries, but the Puyallup do, and combine them with blackcaps.[232] The Quileute also use the vine with the leaves attached, either fresh or dried for tea as a beverage. The Cowlitz make a similar tea for which they claim no medicinal value. In Haeberlin's notes, "gudbix[u]" is listed for blackberry; the similarity in name leads to the belief that this berry was meant. Its use is the same as that of the Puyallup.[233]

Medicine. The Skagit use the leaves for a tea to aid stomach trouble. The Snohomish have no medicinal use for the plant.

Rubus laciniatus Willd. Evergreen Blackberry (adventive).

This plant was discussed only with the Cowlitz informant, who distinguished it from the other varieties of *Rubus* and pointed out that it is used only fresh and the berries are never dried.

This variety is included by Reagan in his eight varieties of *Rubus*; he locates it around Oberg's place and in the vicinity of Beaver. He does not recognize it as a recent introduction nor does he comment on the use of all of these berries for canning as a very modern use.

Rubus sp. Blackberry.

In the literature there are a few references to *Rubus* which cannot be identified beyond the species, as with Lower Chinook. According to Eells, the Klallam use the roots of blackberry as a medicine for colds.[234] The Quinault, who call blackberries swaha's, use the berries as they do huckleberries.[235] The medicinal value of the *Rubus* family as an astringent, especially for diarrhoea, as cited by Youngken,[236] does not appear to be known to the Indians.

Fragaria chiloensis (L.) Duch. Wild Strawberry.

Makah	xadī'tap
Quileute	tobīa''a'put, plant; tobī'a, berry; "pick-them-up berries"
Quinault	ts'xĕ'xe'em

Food. The Makah[237] eat the berries fresh, and usually do it in picnic fashion. Parties of women and children go out to the fields of strawberries to pick and eat them right there. They say that this custom developed because the berries are too small and soft to transport. The Quinault also use strawberries as party food, served especially by young women to their guests. The Quileute take the berries home to eat after fish.

Medicine. The Quileute chew the leaves and spit them on burns.

Literature. Reagan gives the Quileute names for strawberry: tsa-e-bah; chilts-shalts-tse-tut, to-be-yah; the last has close resemblance to the one given above. He mentions that the strawberry is common to untimbered, non-swampy places, especially on the coast. Reagan speaks of the preserving of strawberries, a use not mentioned by modern informants.[238] Stuhr lists the fruit as a refrigerant, esculent.[239]

Fragaria bracteata Heller. Wild Strawberry.

Cowlitz	suspana's, plant; suspa'n, berry
Swinomish	tcī''ox

A specimen of this variety was obtained from the Cowlitz, who use the berry fresh and dried, the only exception to the statement made above in connection with Reagan. They also say that bears and birds eat the fruit. The leaves are used for a beverage, not a medicinal tea. The Swinomish use the berry fresh only. They use the same name for the cultivated berry.

Fragaria cuneifolia Nutt. Wild Strawberry.

Chehalis	tca'tisa
Klallam	tĕ'ĕ'uk, plant; taiyū'qwīltc, berry
Squaxin	t'ĕ'lakwats, plant; t'e'lakw, berry

Food. While the specimen discussed was the *cuneifolia*, the informant said the same name is applied by the Klallam to all varieties of strawberries: in short, they recognize the presence of several species, but do not distinguish them by separate names. All the groups mentioned above eat the berry fresh.

Fragaria sp.

Puyallup-Nisqually	t'e'lɑq[u]
Skokomish	t!a''qwĕ

These people often mash the strawberry before eating it. They also dry the berry but realize that it loses most of its substance in the process.[240] The Lower Chinook eat the berry fresh. Berries are eaten in walking along by the Skokomish. They also boil the whole plant as a tea for diarrhoea.

[231] Ballard.
[232] Smith, pp. 249, 247-48.
[233] Haeberlin and Gunther, p. 21.
[234] Eells, p. 617.
[235] Olson, p. 54.
[236] Youngken, p. 373.
[237] Also cited by Densmore, p. 320.
[238] Reagan, p. 63.
[239] Stuhr, p. 118.
[240] Smith, p. 249.

Potentilla pacifica Howell. (*Argentina pacifica* (Howell) Rydb.) Silverweed.

| Makah | ki'chapi[241] |
| Quileute | g'xēwa'atsod, "just straight down," k'lik'li·'cit |

Food. The woman Quileute informant gave the first of the names listed above, while the man gave the other. They agree on the use of its root as food. It is steamed and dipped in whale oil before eating. A specimen was shown to the Squaxin and Swinomish informants, but was not known to them.

Literature. In connection with this plant, popularly known as silverweed or cinque foil, Haskins gives a quotation which is long enough and in such characteristic style that it could be traced. On p. 184, the quotation beginning: "This is the cinquefoil that holds a prominent place in the tales. . ." is from Boas, "Ethnology of the Kwakiutl," RBAE 35:618.[242] Swan also mentions the use of silverweed by the Lower Chinook.[243]

Potentilla gracilis Dougl. Silverweed or Cinquefoil.

This species was identified only from the Chehalis. The informant knew no name for it, but described this use: the plant has both yellow and white flowers, so a woman wishing to bear a girl drinks tea made from a plant with yellow flowers, and to bear a boy uses the white flowered plant the same way. The same specimen was shown to the Squaxin informant, who did not recognize it.

Geum macrophyllum Willd. Yellow Avens.

Chehalis	t'sit'sialk'um, "a prairie that sings"
Klallam	ngkłał, "green medicine"
Quileute	ko·'lukwł, "it makes your skin break"
	xatalītcixł, "hair seal leaves"
Quinault	xwoili'nst'ont
Snohomish	tsabiłtc

Medicine. Wherever this plant is used, its astringent qualities are recognized. The Snohomish put the leaves on boils, as do the Quileute. The Quinault smash the leaves and rub them on open cuts. Its other use is in connection with childbirth. The Quileute chew the leaves during labor, because they are found at the birth of seal pups, according to Quileute tradition. The Klallam use it in the same way. The Chehalis women steep the leaves and drink the tea to avoid further conception. This can be used only after some children have been born. It is a question whether this should be classified as a medicine or a charm.

This plant was not known to the Cowlitz and Squaxin. The Snohomish informant confused it with fringe-cup (*Tellima grandiflora*) and gave both plants the same name.

Literature. Stuhr states that the roots and rhizomes are astringent and probably have medicinal values.[244] The leaves are used in the instances listed above.

Prunus emarginata (Dougl.) Walp. Wild Cherry.

Green River	pūlē'lad, pipɛlā'lad, "little ones"
Quinault	pīlĕ''la
Skokomish	yilia'lpē
Snohomish	plai'la
Swinomish	plē'lats
Upper Skagit	plē'ba''ats; plĕ''la, cherries

Materials. Two Quinault women contradicted each other on the use of cherry bark on imbricated baskets. It is, however, used in tying the prongs of the fish spears. The Snohomish and all the other Puget Sound tribes who make imbricated baskets use the cherry bark in the imbricated design. It is also used in wrapping many implements, such as fish spears and fire drills.

Medicine. The Lummi chew the bark to facilitate childbirth. On somewhat the same principle, the bark is boiled and the liquid drunk by the Quinault[245] as a laxative, by the Upper Skagit and Skokomish for a cold. Not quite in the class of a medicine is the use by the same people of rotten cherry wood mixed with water and drunk as a contraceptive.

Literature. Stuhr lists *P. serotina* Ehr. as having the same properties attributed to the *emarginata* above. He makes no mention of the species *emarginata*.[246]

Osmaronia cerasiformis (T. and G.) Greene. Oso Berry, Squaw Plum, Indian Plum.

Chehalis	t'saxwanł, whole plant; t'saxwa', berries
Cowlitz	t'skwani'yas, whole plant; tmuc, berries
Lummi	molxwu'n
Quinault	tĕkadja'nt, "coffee berries"
Samish	t'sxuni'ltc
Skagit	siqwad
Snohomish	s'qwa'da'ts
Squaxin	t'sxwa'dats, plant; t'sa'xwad, berries
Swinomish	t'sxwa'dats

Food. The Cowlitz dry the berries for winter use, as well as eating them fresh. The Samish and Swinomish eat the berries fresh. The Chehalis informant stated that if one ate too many berries, one's mouth would turn black, and one would get stomach ache. The Squaxin eat the berries, but do not consider them very good. The Quinault, Skagit, Lummi, and Snohomish eat the berries fresh.

Literature. Reagan states that this bush is rather common but not used very much by the Indians.[247] In the listings above indicating that the berries were

---

[241] Densmore has listed *Potentilla anserina* L. which is not included by Jones in the *Potentilla* found on the Olympic Peninsula. It is called ki'chapi by the Makah and the roots are eaten. Densmore, p. 320.

[242] Haskins, p. 184.

[243] Swan, *Northwest Coast*, p. 88.

[244] Stuhr, p. 118.

[245] Olson, p. 181.

[246] Stuhr, No. 966.

[247] Reagan, p. 64.

eaten, I gathered that they were casually picked in walking through the woods, or resorted to in starvation periods.

Amelanchier florida Lindl. Serviceberry.

Chehalis	k'wɑla'stam, berries
Klallam	tcetci'ntc
Lummi	s'tcɪ'tsɛn
Samish	steitcsɛn, name of the wood of this plant
Skagit	qwɪla'stɑp
Snohomish	k!ola'stabats
Swinomish	qula'stabats, name of the wood of this plant

Food. The Swinomish eat the fruit fresh and dry it for winter use, as do the Chehalis, who use the dried berries as seasoning in soup or with meats. The Skagit eat the berries fresh and state that the Yakima dry them. The Lummi dry the berries and boil them in winter with dog salmon at feasts. The Snohomish, Klallam, and Lower Chinook[248] also relish the fruit.

Materials. The Snohomish use the wood of this plant for discs for slahalem, one of the local gambling games. These discs are about the diameter of a silver dollar, and twice as thick. The Samish and Swinomish exploit the toughness of this wood in using it as the spreader in the rigging of the halibut line. Even a large halibut could not break this.

Pyrus diversifolia Bong. Crab Apple.

Cowlitz	ku'mtlas, plant; kumł, fruit
Green River	ka''ax·ᵘ
Makah	tup!kɑ'bupt, plant; tsɪxa'pix, apple
Quileute	syuyu'xkidax, tree; syuyu'kidaxput, fruit, "it hurts your tongue"
Quinault	qwě'tsunixlak, fruit
Samish	qa'xwiltc
Swinomish	qa·'xwats

Food. The Swinomish, Samish, and Quileute eat the fruit raw, while the Makah, Quinault, Lower Chinook, and Cowlitz all soften the fruit by storing it in baskets. The Cowlitz cook the fruit a little first, before storing it.

Materials. The Quileute make the prongs of the seal spear of this wood, because of its lightness in weight and toughness. It is also used for a maul for driving stakes and as bait lure on a sea-bass hook.

Medicine. For medicinal purposes, the bark is considered most potent. It is peeled and soaked in water which is drunk by the Makah for intestinal disorders, dysentery, and diarrhoea.[249] They also chew it and put it on wounds. The Klallam and the Quinault use the same infusion as an eye wash. When this combination is boiled it is drunk by the

Quinault to cure "any soreness inside, for it goes all through the blood." The Swinomish and Samish boil the bark and use the brew to wash out cuts and take it internally for stomach disorders. The Quileute take bark from a tree growing on any island like James Island or Destruction Island, and make a tea which is drunk for lung trouble. For this purpose the Makah chew the leaves, which have been soaked in water. They are very bitter, and make one "feel drunk."

Miscellaneous. Mr. Ballard reports that the Green River people say the pheasants and grouse feed on the wild crab apples and some say that the bears do also.

Literature. Reagan mentions specific places in the Quileute territory where wild crab apples grow in abundance: at the head of the Hoh River, and in the swampy region east of the old Wesley Smith schoolhouse. He says that the tea was used as a remedy for gonorrhea.[250] Haskins, without naming the tribe, states that one use of crab apple is for wedges, reminiscent of its use as mauls for driving stakes, found among the Quileute.[251] Menzies saw wild crab apple trees at Port Discovery, May 2, 1792.[252] Swan mentions the abundant growth of crab apples in the Willapa Harbor region, and the fact that the Lower Chinook used them.[253] No information regarding this plant is found in any of the pharmaceutical books consulted.

LEGUMINOSAE. Pea Family

Lupinus bicolor Lindl. Lupine.

A specimen of this plant was secured in Chehalis territory and shown to Chehalis and Squaxin informants but they knew no name for it and said it was not used.

Lupinus polyphyllus Lindl. Lupine.

This was obtained in Cowlitz territory, but was not recognized by a Cowlitz informant.

Lupinus littoralis Dougl.

This was identified by the Lower Chinook as the plant whose root they roast in hot embers and then pound to loosen the edible fibers from the spine.[254]

Literature. Lupine is often mentioned by the early travelers, but of course the variety is not given.

Trifolium fimbriatum Lindl. Beach Clover.

A specimen of this plant was found only in Makah territory on this survey, though Jones lists it in many other places on the Olympic Peninsula. The Makah call it k!ôxtap and steam the roots for eating.[255]

248 Miss Louise Colbert.
249 Densmore, p. 315, cites a decoction of bark for boils, sores, and bleeding piles. It is also a tonic.
250 Reagan, p. 64.
251 Haskins, p. 161.
252 Menzies, p. 20.
253 Swan, *Northwest Coast*, p. 89.
254 Ray, p. 119.
255 According to Densmore, p. 319, this plant was found on Tatoosh Island and eaten as food.

Vicia sativa L. Spring Vetch.

This vetch was found in the Skagit region in June and was identified by the informant as tcitcila′xwats, "mountain peas." She said bears like it, but her people do not use it.

Vicia angustifolia (L.) Reichard. Narrow-leaved Vetch.

Only one specimen of this was secured. A Snohomish informant identified it as tcitci′laxwads, the same as the spring vetch of the Skagit. She said the plant is soaked in water and is used hot on the hair for headache.

Vicia gigantea Hook. Giant Vetch.

Makah	tcatcapatsaklĭ′bupt, "canoe plant" (because the pods are shaped like canoes)[256]
Quileute	babīdaqwu′tput, "pretty nearly like string beans"
Quinault	manuxkuxtostɑp

Materials. The Makah use the leaves and vines to cover sprouts while they are steaming.[257]

Medicine, Charms. The roots are soaked and the water used as a hair wash by the Makah. The Quinault woman rubs herself with the roots, wraps them up, and puts them under her pillow if her husband has left her.[258] This will bring him back. Sometimes a deserted husband may do the same.

Literature. Haskins states that the seeds of this vetch are edible and used by the Indians, but no such use was found here.

It may be noted that the Quileute word for this vetch compares it to string beans, a recent introduction. They say that this vetch also is used in their region, but know no specific use.

Vicia americana Muhl. Vetch.

| Chehalis | ubq′ε′łtnł |
| Squaxin | lipwa′hats, plant; lipwa′, peas |

Medicine. The Squaxin crush the leaves in bath water to take away soreness.

Miscellaneous. The Chehalis do not use the plant, but know that deer and mountain beaver eat it.

Lotus micranthus Benth. (*Hosackia parviflora* Benth.) Lotus.

A specimen of this was shown to a Chehalis informant, who recognized it as "something wild," but knew no name or use for it.

GERANIACEAE. Geranium Family

Geranium pusillum Burm. f. Low Geranium.

This plant is listed by Jones as a common weed in lawns and cultivated ground, and is included in his list of adventitious plants appearing before 1900.[259]

It was not known to the Cowlitz informant to whom it was shown.

Geranium molle L.

This geranium, also listed by Jones as an adventitious plant and also as a common weed on lawns,[260] is called swi′tkin by the Chehalis, but not used. The Squaxin do not know it.

OXALIDACEAE. Oxalis or Wood-sorrel Family

Oxalis oregana Nutt. Wood-sorrel.

Cowlitz	tcna″ai
Makah	chaiba′kcun, "sour"[261] tcaiba′kcun
Quileute	ka′a·′lats or k'e′a′xłatsput
Quinault	qwoi′ĕts′stap, "sour"

Food. The Cowlitz eat the leaves fresh or cooked and say they taste "just like apples." The Quileute, who regard the leaves as slightly bitter, say that hunters or those traveling in the woods eat them as they walk along. The Quinault use them as we do wilted lettuce, cooking them with grease. The informant drew this parallel.

Medicine. The fresh juice is squeezed from the plant and applied to sore eyes by the Cowlitz, while the Quinault chew the roots and then squeeze them into the eyes. The Quileute wilt the leaves and put them on boils to draw them. According to Densmore the Makah boil some in a little water as a remedy for "summer complaint."[262]

Literature. It is mentioned by Stuhr that the plant contains acid potassium oxalate.[263]

ACERACEAE. Maple Family

Acer macrophyllum Pursh. Broadleaf Maple, Oregon Maple.

Chehalis	k′u′ławi, tree
Cowlitz	cuk′ums
Klallam	stsła″atc
Lummi	k!amali′tc
Skokomish	k!o′łūwĕ
Snohomish	stcō′klats
Squaxin	t′cu·′lats
Swinomish	tci′oxłklats

Materials. Next to the conifers, the maples—both *macrophyllum* (broadleaf) and *circinatum* (vine maple) are perhaps the most useful trees in the Northwest. The Cowlitz use the bark in making rope and tumplines. The leaves are used by the Skagit, Lummi, and Snohomish to cover food cooking in pits, and are especially mentioned in connection with cooking elderberries for storage by the Snohomish and Skagit. The Squaxin, however, believe that maple leaves are too strong to use in baking pits, but use the leaves to lay fish on while cleaning them.

---

[256] Densmore, p. 320, records the Makah name as chicha, patsaklibup, meaning "plant-bearing moss."
[257] Densmore, p. 320.
[258] Densmore, p. 320, states that the Makah girls who want to attract boys rub themselves with the pounded root.
[259] Jones, pp. 189, 56.

[259] Jones, p. 56.
[251] Densmore, pp. 310, 313.
[262] Densmore, p. 313.
[263] Stuhr, p. 100.

The dead wood is used by the Swinomish for smoking salmon. The Chehalis and Quinault also use it for this purpose. The Nisqually cover temporary houses with the boughs.

The wood of the maple is one of the most useful in the Northwest for carving. Many of the very beautiful wood-carvings of the Haida, Tlingit, and Tsimshian are made of maple. In this part of the Northwest its value is also realized, and it is used for carving dugout bowls, dishes, platters, and spoons by the Quinault.[264] The Lummi make the framework for the sweatlodge of maple.[265] The Klallam, Snohomish, and Skagit make canoe paddles of it. In addition to paddles, the Swinomish use it for cradle boards, dishes, and spoons. The Lummi use it the same way. The Skokomish have many similar uses for the wood, which the informant did not enumerate.

Medicine. The only medicinal use of maple recorded is for the Klallam, who boil the bark and drink the infusion for tuberculosis.

Literature. Menzies records maple at Port Discovery, May, 1792.[266] Stuhr states that the medicinal properties are doubtful and the use of maple uncertain.[267] Reagan gives the word hkats-to-ah-put for the Quileute and says that the tree is very common and the wood widely used.[268]

Acer circinatum Pursh. Vine Maple.

Chehalis	p'a·'niɫ
Klallam	pakɫtc
Lummi	t!ɛkaiyɛxɫp
Quileute	t'u'psiyu'q'pat, "it splits easily"
Quinault	maxo"atcaɫnix, "basket tree"
Skagit	tak'tak'ka'ts
Snohomish	kɛpkɪ'wats
Swinomish	tɛtɛka'ts

Materials. The fact that the Quinault refer to this as the "basket tree" indicates one of its widespread uses. Its long straight shoots are appreciated for making an openwork basket with a crossed-warp twine or a broad-spaced checker board weave. These baskets are used for general household utility, such as carrying wood, clams, and fish. The Quinault[269] use vine maple for the wattleworks of fish traps, as do the Chehalis, Quileute, and Lummi; the Quinault also use poles of vine maple to hold down the roof planks on houses. The Skagit use saplings as swings for babies' cradles. They also make salmon tongs of it. In many places it is used for firewood, and the Quinault use the charcoal to mix with oil for black paint. The Skokomish informant only knew that the wood was used.

Vine maple was not known to the Squaxin informant.

---

[264] Olson, pp. 80, 81.
[265] Stern, p. 35.
[266] Menzies, p. 20.
[267] Stuhr, p. 11.
[268] Reagan, p. 65.
[269] Olson, pp. 28, 36, 62.

Literature. Reagan gives as the Quileute word top'tse-yo-kas-put, closely resembling the one given by the modern informant, and states that maple is widely used.[270]

RHAMNACEAE. Buckthorn Family

Rhamnus Purshiana DC. Cascara.

Cowlitz	k'lɑta'ni
Green River	tl'awa'da'ts
Klallam	wū'cinūtc
Lummi	k'aiyeɫp
Makah	k!labuq!wacbupt
Quileute	aqi'lipat, "bear berry plant"; aqi'l, bear
Quinault	xwixwi'niɫ; maxa'akten, "have bowel movement"
Skagit	tatsa'bats
Upper Skagit	xɫats
Squaxin	k'ladyats
Swinomish	tatsa'bats

Food. The Makah eat the berries fresh in July and August. The Quileute believe the pheasants eat them and that it makes their meat better.

Materials. The Skagit boil the bark for green dye on mountain-goat wool.

Medicine. The bark is universally used as a laxative, but there are other uses given also. The Squaxin use the infusion to wash sores and also chew the bark and spit it on sores. The Skagit burn the bark and mix the charcoal with grease and rub it on swellings. Densmore lists a decoction of a handful of the inner bark to a quart of water, as a remedy for dysentery.[271]

Literature. Reagan calls the plant ak-ke-le, which the modern informant gave as the word from which the plant name was derived. The Quileute, according to Reagan, used this plant as the remedy for many diseases. He mentioned the fact that overdoses were often given and occasionally fatal.[272] All the pharmaceutical books list the same uses of cascara as those found among the Indians. They also give Oregon, Washington, and northern California as the regions from which the largest commercial supply is shipped. The plant is named for the German, Fred Pursh, and was introduced into modern medicine by Dr. J. H. Bundy in 1877.[273] *Rhamnus* was seen at Dabob Bay by Menzies on May 12, 1792.[274]

VIOLACEAE. Violet Family

Viola adunca Sm. (*V. retroscabra* Piper Fl. Wash.) Yellow Violet.

This plant was shown to both Klallam and Makah informants, who gave uses for it but did not know their own names for it. The Makah women eat the

---

[270] Reagan, p. 65.
[271] Densmore, p. 314.
[272] Reagan, p. 65.
[273] Gathercoal and Wirth, p. 452.
[274] Menzies, p. 28.

roots and leaves during labor. The Klallam mash the flowers and lay them on the chest or side for pain. They are left on only two or three hours, because they blister the skin.

CACTACEAE. Cactus Family

Opuntia sp.

This entry is not made from an identified specimen. In his account of the Lummi, Stern states that they singe the sharp points off a cactus, mash it, soak it in salt water, and drink this liquid to facilitate childbirth.[275] Since *Opuntia* is the only cactus found in western Washington, it is probably the one Stern mentioned. Jones repeats the entry of Menzies, who was "surprised to meet with the cactus *opuntia*."[276]

ELAEAGNACEAE. Oleaster Family

Shepherdia canadensis (L.) Nutt. (*Lepargyrea canadensis* (L.) Greene.) Buffalo-berry, Soapberry.

This plant was identified only by the Makah, who call it patsa'p'ats. It does not grow at Neah Bay, according to the informant. The berries are whipped into a froth which is used as a dessert at feasts.

ONAGRACEAE. Evening-primrose Family

Epilobium angustifolium L. (*E. spicatum* Lam.) Fireweed.

Klallam	sɪ''ɛltc
Makah	popoxsa'dix, "feather plant"
Skagit	xa'ctats
Skokomish	sp!ukosai
Snohomish	xa'tc'tats
Swinomish	χa'tctɑts

Materials. Among most Puget Sound people who wove mountain-goat-wool blankets, the cotton of the fireweed was used to fill out the supply of wool. The Quinault and Skokomish combined this cotton with duck feathers for blankets.

Medicine. The Swinomish boil the whole plant and bathe invalids in the liquid. It is poisonous to drink. The Snohomish boil the root and use the infusion as a remedy for sore throat; the Skokomish drink it for tuberculosis.

Miscellaneous. Fireweed is so plentiful in burnt-over and logged-off areas that it is hard to realize its former limited range. The Quileute and Cowlitz informants did not recognize the plant. The Makah, who do not use it, give it the same name, "feather plant," which they use for *Eriophorum*.

ARALIACEAE. Aralia Family

Oplopanax horridum (Sm.) Miquel. (*Echinopanax horridum* (Sm.) Dcne. & Planch.) Devil's Club.

Cowlitz	sqaipqa'ipas
Green River	xaxadɪ'a'ts[277]

Klallam	pŏkltc
Lummi	qwu'n'numpł
Skagit	xadɪ'ats
Snuqualmi	tcitca'tcɪlụ''i[278]
Swinomish	xadɪ'ats

Materials. Sticks of devil's club are burned by the Lummi and mixed with grease for face paint. It gives a reddish brown. Today it is still used, but mixed with vaseline instead of grease. The Klallam peel a stick and cut it into small pieces, which are fastened to bass lines. Under water it releases itself and spins to the surface, and the fish follows it.

Medicine. The Cowlitz cut the thorns off and peel the bark. It is boiled, and the infusion drunk for a cold or used to wash a limb affected with rheumatism. They also dry the bark and pulverize it, to be used as a perfume or baby talc. The Cowlitz regard the plant as poison and believe that stickers from it may cause inflammation.[279] The Green River people, according to Mr. Ballard, steep the roots and use the liquid for colds. They also dry the bark and pulverize it as a deodorant. The Skagit use this plant in combination with others, a procedure which is very rare in this body of medicinal knowledge. They boil the bark and root with Princess pine and cascara bark and drink the brew for tuberculosis. The Skagit also drink this tea to reestablish regular menstrual flow after childbirth. The Lummi cut the thorns off and lay the bark on a woman's breast to stop an excessive flow of milk.

Literature. Haskins speaks of the widespread use of this plant on the coast as a medicine, as a charm for fishing, and an emetic. Perhaps if the references were given, this information could be traced. The plant is not easy to find and handle, and so it was not shown to informants as often as many others. Perhaps more information can still be obtained.

UMBELLIFERAE. Parsley Family

Sanicula Menziesii Hook. & Arn.

This specimen was shown to only one informant, a Chehalis, who did not recognize it.

Osmorhiza chilensis (H. & A. Bot. Beechey Voy. 26 :1830) *Washingtonia brevipes.* Sweet Cicely.

Skagit	sq!ŏlŏbyū'yū'batc, "butterfly cooking"
Swinomish	kŏks'kĕca't

Miscellaneous. The plant was not known to the Lummi informant. The Skagit do not use the plant, but they say that the butterflies always eat on it when it is blooming. Only the Swinomish give any use for this plant, and they chew the root as a very powerful love charm.

[275] Stern, p. 14.
[276] Jones, p. 194.
[277] Ballard.

[278] *Idem.*
[279] This agrees with the statement by Muenscher, p. 169.

Heracleum lanatum Michx.   Cow Parsnip.

Makah	kĭ'stop
Quileute	k'lōpi't
Quinault	waka', "kills the pain"

Food. The young tops are eaten raw in the spring by the Makah, and later the stems are also eaten. The Lower Chinook eat the young stems, after peeling the outer skin.[280] The Quileute dip the young stems in seal oil when eating them, as do the Quinault.

Materials. The Quileute and Makah girls make baskets of the large blossoms of the cow parsnip, by twining the stems of the blossoms with sea weed. They fill the baskets with shells for playing. The Quileute call such a basket k'lūp'itbai.

Medicine. The leaves are warmed and put on sore limbs by the Quinault.

Literature. Reagan mentions the use of cow parsnip as a favorite spring-tonic food,[281] while Haskins says that it was eaten from Alaska to California. In this reference, the use of ashes from burnt stalks as a substitute for salt is mentioned, and it would be very interesting to know which tribe used this.[282] Swan's record of the Shoalwater Bay people agrees with Ray's present-day account.[283] Stuhr also comments on the use of this plant by the Indians as food. He also states that the roots and leaves are acrid, irritant, and poisonous;[284] perhaps their application to sore limbs by the Quinault was in the nature of a counter-irritant.

Conium maculatum L.   Poison Hemlock.

| Klallam | sakᵘqwuk'ka'in |
| Snohomish | ceukceu'k |

Charms. The roots of this plant are poisonous[285] but bring good luck in various ways. The Snohomish rub it on their fish hooks, so the fish won't smell the fisherman. The Klallam woman who wishes to attract the attention of a man will rub her body with this root after bathing. This plant is an old one here, according to this informant, but Jones lists it among the plants introduced since the beginning of the twentieth century.[286] Stuhr also states that it escaped from cultivation.[287]

Oenanthe sarmentosa Presl.   Water Parsley or Wild Celery.

Cowlitz	x̣tsx̣u'ts
Makah	wawakĭ'xbupt, "frog plant"
Skokomish	sp!ai'yeputsai
Snuqualmi	sqwu'labts, "Indian celery"

Food. The Cowlitz eat the stems while they are young and tender, as do the Lower Chinook,[288] Snuqualmi,[289] and Skokomish.

Materials. The stalks at a later stage are cut and used as whistles by the children, among the Makah and Quileute.

Medicine. The Makah pound the root between stones and use it as a laxative, which is said to be very potent.

Literature. Stuhr reports the plant as poisonous.[290]

CORNACEAE.   Dogwood Family

Cornus pubescens (Nutt.) Coville.   (*C. occidentalis* (T. & G.) Coville.)

| Green River | pakpₐki', tree; tsₐ'tsx, berry |
| Snohomish | s'tcī"ūwxsats |

Medicine. The Snohomish scrape the bark and boil it. This infusion is used on sore eyes.

Miscellaneous. The Green River people wash away the outer pulp of the berry and chew the kernel. They say the berries are eaten by bears.

Cornus Nuttallii Audubon.   Nuttall's or Pacific Flowering Dogwood.

Green River	kuda'bĭt[291]
Klallam	slaxalemĭltc
Lummi	qwĕ'txĕltc
Skagit	kłō'bats, tree; kłoba'ts'sĭbiau, "eye of coyote," blossom
Snohomish	sta'idjoqwads
Snuqualmi	t'adjo"qwats[291]
Swinomish	t'ɛt'ɛk'ɛka'ts

Materials. The Quinault use the charcoal for tattooing. There is no dogwood near Taholah, but they find it on the way to Oakville. The Green River tribe, the Skagit, and the Klallam use the wood for making discs for the gambling game, slahalem, a hiding-the-ball game. Because dogwood, according to the Skagit, becomes a hard wood after it dries, its use for foreshafts of salmon harpoons is logical. The Snohomish make sticks of dogwood to pound brake ferns after roasting.

Medicine. The Lummi peel the bark and boil it as a laxative. The Green River people use it as a physic and emetic.

Literature. Reagan gives several uses of dogwood by the Quileute not found among the other local groups. The berries of this dogwood and also *C. canadensis* are used in ceremonies. He mentions the use of the bark as a tonic tea, similar to the Green River and Lummi uses. To call the dried leaves (which, when smoked, gave an intoxicating effect) "kinnikinnick" is, I believe, an error, for usually "kinnikinnick" is the name for *Arctostaphylos Uva-ursi*, although it might be applied to any dried leaves which are smoked.[292]

Haskins states the following: "Townsend, on his journey to Oregon in 1833, reports marked success in

[280] Ray, p. 121.
[281] Reagan, p. 68.
[282] Haskins, p. 235.
[283] Swan, *Northwest Coast*, p. 87.
[284] Stuhr, p. 137.
[285] Listed as *Cicuta maculatum* by Muenscher, p. 170.
[286] Jones, p. 56.
[287] Stuhr, p. 136.
[288] Ray, p. 123.
[289] The informant was not sure of the difference between this and "hemlock."
[290] Stuhr, p. 138.
[291] Ballard.
[292] Reagan, p. 66.

curing Indian children of malaria through its use. The bark is bitter and tonic and has been used successfully in place of quinine."[293]

Cornus canadensis L. Bunchberry.

Makah	būbūkwak!tibupt, "berries with pebbles in them"; būbūkwak!lt, berries
Quinault	olka'stap, snakeberry

Food. The Makah eat the berries fresh, but the Quinault declare they are poisonous.

Literature. Haskins states that the berries, though insipid, are edible and are used by the Indians of the coast of British Columbia.[294]

ERICACEAE. Heath Family

Monotropa uniflora L. Indian Pipe.

Indian pipe was found in the Makah territory, but the informant did not know its name or use.

Ledum groenlandicum Oeder. Labrador Tea.

Makah	būpesbupt (same name as cranberry, because they always grow together)
Quinault	nūwaqwa'ntI, "prairie tea"

Food. The leaves are steeped and drunk as a beverage tea by the Makah.

Medicine. A stronger infusion is used by the Makah as a blood purifier. The Quinault use the same drink for rheumatism.

Miscellaneous. The Klallam, like the Makah, note the presence of Labrador tea with cranberry and use the same name for it. The Klallam informant knew this fact but could not recall the name.

Literature. Stuhr and the U.S. Dispensatory mention the Labrador tea as a tonic, expectorant, and pectoral.[295]

Rhododendron albiflorum Hook. Rhododendron.

This is listed for only one tribe, the Skokomish, because it was never available for discussion elsewhere. They call it xawxu'ptɛd, "leaves shaped like paddles," and use the buds boiled in water as a cold and sore-throat medicine. For an ulcerated stomach the buds are chewed and swallowed. They are also chewed and spit on cuts, which are then wrapped in shredded cedar bark.

Menziesia ferruginea Sm. Fool's Huckleberry.

Quileute	ticu kutli'tpet, "bottom sticks"

Materials. The Quileute weave the twigs together with cedar bark for a grill on the bottom of the canoe. This is used by women to sit on.

Charms. The Quinault informant, a woman, could not remember the name of this bush, but she said a woman used to cut a twig with a forked end, about two feet long, and carry it, waving it in the air and singing a song to make a man fall in love with her. Only women did this.

Gaultheria Shallon Pursh. Salal.

Klallam	t!a'ka
Makah	sala'xbupt
Quileute	ko'o'·d;[296] ku'u'd, plant; ku'u'dpat, berries
Quinault	kwa'soitcnu'l, the bush; bu'tskitl, leaves; kwa'soitcɛn, skwasa'utca·n[297]
Samish	ta'qa
Skagit	ta"kats, plant; ta'ka, berries
Skokomish	t!a'xka
Snohomish	ta'ka"ats
Swinomish	ta'qa·ts

Food. Wherever the berries of the salal are used, they are mashed and dried in cakes, often put on split cedar boards or on skunk cabbage leaves. These cakes are soaked to prepare them for eating and are dipped in whale or seal oil. The Quileute pick the whole twig with the berries and, dipping it in whale oil, pull it through the mouth to eat the berries while they are still fresh. The loaves of salal berries prepared by the Lower Chinook weigh as much as 10 to 15 pounds. When the berries are dried, the Skokomish work fresh ones into them as binder before forming them into cakes.

Materials. Large leaves are used to line food cooking pits and under drying berries.

Medicine. The Klallam chew the leaves and spit them on burns; the Quileute use the same treatment on sores. The Swinomish and Samish also use the leaves in tea form to cure a cough or tuberculosis. The Quinault chew the leaves to relieve heartburn and colic, according to one informant, and another stated that the leaves were also boiled and the juice drunk for diarrhoea. The Skagit use a mild form of this tea for a convalescent tonic.

Miscellaneous. The Makah dry, pulverize, and smoke these leaves with kinnikinnick, according to the present-day informant and also according to Swan.[298]

Literature. Reagan lists this plant as "kood-put," and mentions its food value and also the use of its roots and bark for medicinal purposes, a fact not verified in the present study. He records that the Quileute used it for smoking in the manner listed here only for the Makah. The salal brush, according to Reagan, is used in the "Klukwalle" dances, another fact which was not mentioned by the present-day informants, perhaps on account of lack of knowledge of the rituals.[299]

[293] Haskins, p. 241.
[294] Haskins, p. 241.
[295] Stuhr, p. 59; U.S. Dispensatory, p. 1362.
[296] Andrade, p. 164.
[297] Olson, p. 54.
[298] Swan, *Indians of Cape Flattery*, p. 27.
[299] Reagan, p. 67.

The pharmacognosies state that all species of the heath family contain tannic and gallic acid. In the light of this statement, the use of the chewed leaves on burns is a proper medical practice.

Arbutus Menziesii Pursh. Madrona.

It has been most unfortunate that the madrona has not been available more often where these field studies have been made. It was discussed with the Skokomish informant, who called it tsɪ' xwēxē and said the leaves are boiled and the infusion drunk for colds, sore throat, or ulcerated stomach. Sometimes Oregon grape roots or licorice are added. Reagan mentions that the Quileute smoked the leaves.[300] Stuhr states that an astringent infusion made of the bark, root, and leaves is used by "the Indians" for a cold.[301]

Arctostaphylos Uva-ursi (L.) Spreng. Kinnikinnick.

Chehalis	kaya'nɬ
Klallam	kinnikinnick
Makah	kwɪca'
Skokomish	sk!ēwat
Squaxin	s'qaya'dats

Food. While the Chehalis say the berries are too seedy and have no taste, the Squaxin occasionally eat them. The Lower Chinook use them as a regular item of diet, eating them fresh or mixed with oil after they have been dried in bags. The Skokomish eat the berries with salmon eggs.

Miscellaneous. Much more uniform is the use of the leaves of kinnikinnick as the principal smoking mixture of the Northwest. Before the introduction of tobacco, the leaves were pulverized and smoked alone. Later they were used to stretch the small supplies of tobacco available. The Chehalis say if one swallows the smoke of kinnikinnick, it produces a drunken feeling. The Klallam informant said that either kinnikinnick or yew leaves were mixed with tobacco, but kinnikinnick was never mixed with yew because it was too strong.

Literature. All the early observers commented on the presence of kinnikinnick. Swan mentions it twice for the Lower Chinook and the Quinault, and adds the custom of swallowing smoke to stupefy the smoker.[302] Reagan, a more recent writer, gives the following account: "Some years ago an Indian of the Quillayute tribe got intoxicated by smoking *A. Uva-ursi* leaves and danced in the fire barefooted till the soles of his feet were burned to a crisp and his feet deformed for life. Some years previous another old Indian got drunk on the narcotic inhaled while smoking the leaves of this plant. As a result of being drunk, he fell in the fire, burned his feet almost off, burned his hands badly, also burned his nose completely off, also a part of his lips. In this condition he lived many years."[303]

Vaccinium ovatum Pursh. Evergreen Huckleberry.

This species was collected only once during these field trips, but is mentioned often in the literature. Olson lists it for the Quinault as nakȧ'ltcȧn. The berries are sun- or smoke-dried, partly mashed, pressed into cake form, and wrapped in leaves or bark.[304] The present-day informant called the plant k'wɪ'uxsnɬ, and the berries k'wi'uxs and said the berries were eaten fresh. Reagan called this species blueberry and speaks of "huckleberries and blueberries," obviously not making any distinction between the varieties.[303] Menzies saw this plant at Dabob Bay, May 11, 1792.[305] Ray in his *Lower Chinook Ethnographic Notes* lists references to it in Thwaites, *Journals of Lewis and Clark;* Coues, *The Journals of Alexander Henry and David Thompson;* and Swan, *Northwest Coast.*[306]

Vaccinium ovalifolium Sm. Blue Huckleberry.

Makah	xōxōyak
Quileute	t'uwa·dak[307]
Quinault	sk'iuxsnɬ, "winter huckleberry bushes"

Food. In addition to the tribes listed above, the Klallam and Lower Chinook also use this berry, but the informants did not know its name. Everywhere the berries are eaten fresh and dried. The Klallam always pick theirs along Hood Canal.

Literature. Reagan gives the Quileute name as to-wa-duk and the same information as for the *V. ovatum.*[308] Swan states: "A species of whortleberry called by the Indians 'shotberries' lasts for months fresh if kept cool and dry. Usually they are dried and eaten in spring before the other berries ripen."[309]

Vaccinium parvifolium Sm. Red Huckleberry.

Klallam	pixwɪ'ltc
Lummi	spixᵘ
Makah	xixsɪ'·'ad
Quileute	tixkɬo'utaput, whole plant; tixkɬa'ut, berries
Quinault	to'xlumnix, "combing off the berries"; tu'hlom, "brushing down"; tao'lom[310]
Skagit	stɪtē'xwats, plant; stɪtē'x, berries
Skokomish	tc'xwē'las
Snohomish	tixwɪ'p
Swinomish	tɪtɪxqwats

Food. The berries are eaten by all the tribes listed above, as well as by many other groups in this area. As indicated by the Quinault name, the berries, instead of being picked individually, are brushed or combed off the twigs. The Lower Chinook think the

---

[300] Reagan, p. 66.
[301] Stuhr, p. 57.
[302] Swan, *Northwest Coast*, pp. 88, 155.
[303] Reagan, p. 67.

[304] Olson, p. 54.
[305] Menzies, p. 27.
[306] Ray, p. 122.
[307] Andrade, p. 164.
[308] Reagan, p. 68.
[309] Swan, *Northwest Coast*, p. 89.
[310] Olson, p. 54.

berries are better adapted to eating raw than drying, and the Lummi agree with them. The Quinault also use the leaves for tea. The Skokomish informant said that eating too many of these berries produces boils. Children are not allowed to eat them.

Medicine. The Skagit boil the bark for a tea for colds.

Literature. Reagan gives the following variations of Quileute names for this variety of huckleberries: te-thluwot, te-thlo-ot-put, te-thloh-ohnt.[311]

Vaccinium Oxycoccus L., var. **ovalifolium** Michx. (*Oxycoccus Oxycoccus intermedius* (Gray) Piper.) Cranberry.

Klallam	klēxōxoits
Makah	pap'es
Quinault	asolmix, "prairie berries"

Food. Cranberries are found in bogs both at sea level and in the hills like the Spruce Orchard country above Moclips. In association with them are found Labrador tea and Alaska sedge cotton. The Quinault pick them at Spruce Orchard, the Klallam near Port Townsend.

The berries are usually stored in boxes or baskets until they are soft and brown.

Literature. Swan states that cranberries were plentiful in the Lower Chinook territory and were an item of trade between the Indians and whites.[312]

PRIMULACEAE. Primrose Family
Trientalis latifolia Hook. Star Flower.

A specimen of this was found only in Cowlitz territory, and the informant, who knew no name for it, said that the juice was squeezed into water and used as an eye wash.

OLEACEAE. Olive Family
Fraxinus oregana Nutt. Oregon Ash.

This tree was identified from a specimen in only one instance—among the Cowlitz, who call it numtac and use the wood for canoe paddles and digging sticks. The bark is boiled and the infusion drunk for worms.

The Quinault, according to Olson,[313] also use the wood of the ash for canoe paddles. The present-day informant insisted, on being shown a specimen, that it was not native.

Stuhr states that the Indians of Washington attribute medicinal value to the roots and apply them to flesh wounds received in bear hunts,[314] but of course gives no specific tribe, nor the source of his information, so it is difficult to check it.

CONVOLVULACEAE. Morning-glory Family
Convolvulus Soldanella L. Morning-glory.

The Makah call these flowers la'a'latck, "flowers," and have no specific use for them.

HYDROPHYLLACEAE. Waterleaf Family
Hydrophyllum tenuipes Heller. Waterleaf.

This is familiar only to the Cowlitz, who have two names for it, tci'tkwalo'h or xotxo'ts. They break up the root and eat it.

LABIATAE. Mint Family
Mentha sp. Mint.

Chehalis	k'a'stuk^w, "you have taken it"
Cowlitz	cu'xacu'xa

Medicine. Both tribes use the leaves for a tea used as a cold remedy. The Cowlitz informant said there were two kinds, one very green and "this one." According to Jones, there are three varieties, but the specimen brought in could not be identified beyond the species.

Literature. The medicinal use of mint is familiar even to the layman. Reagan states that the Quileute used it as smelling and rubbing medicine.[315]

Prunella vulgaris L., var. **lanceolata** (Barton) Fern. (*P. vulgaris* of Piper Fl. Wash.) Self Heal.

Chehalis	spa·'qan, "flowers"
Klallam	sintcīqwuxłakē'qwa'itc
Quileute	klot'opbi'x'a'x
Skagit	tsĕkai's
Snohomish	tsĕka'tsub, "flower" (generic term)
Swinomish	sqwī'qwīlōs, "mountain flower"

Medicine. The Quileute use this plant for boils, but the informant did not know the exact way of preparing it because the knowledge had to be bought from its owner. The Quinault also use it for boils, but the procedure is less esoteric; the juice is simply put on the boil.

Beliefs. The Chehalis do not use the flower, but say that when it is not quite open it has a face like a person. The Skagit and Lummi have no specific use for it; the Lummi say it grows where there has been water which has dried off. The Swinomish and Snohomish have no use for the plant. The Klallam informant said this is not the true kĕqwa'itc whose roots they eat, but its step-brother. The use of kinship forms in regard to flowers is interesting.

Stachys ciliata Dougl. (*S. caurina* Piper; *S. ciliata*, var. *Leachiana* Henders.) Hedge Nettle or Woundwort.

Green River-

Puyallup	qwełuxwastsūts, "marriage relation of nettle," i.e., brother-in-law[316]
Makah	ada"babupt, "milk plant"
Quileute	sisibaxłu
Quinault	qwadjudkolum, "sweet suckers"
Skagit	qwolqwa'ltc'talats, "relation by marriage to the nettle"

Food. The Quinault pick the blossoms and suck the honey.

[311] Reagan, p. 68.
[312] Swan, *Northwest Coast*, p. 89.
[313] Olson, p. 71.

[314] Stuhr, p. 90.
[315] Reagan, p. 68.
[316] Ballard.

Materials. The Makah and Quinault use the whole plant to cover steaming sprouts.

Medicine. The Green River and Puyallup people use this plant for healing boils. The Quileute make a steam bath by putting leaves in an alder tub with hot rocks and sitting on it, and cover themselves with elkskin or bearskin.

Beliefs. The Quileute informant said that this plant was indigenous but that the mint, of which there are three varieties, was brought by the whites. The Skagit believe this plant grows with the nettles and pick and use it with them. The Lummi informant could not remember the word in his own language but said they call it the half-brother of the nettle, while both the Skagit and Green River-Puyallup indicate the same marriage relationship.

Marrubium vulgare L. Horehound.

The Cowlitz believe the white people brought it,[317] and while they make no regular use of it, they say it can be used for tea.

SCROPHULARIACEAE. Figwort Family

Verbascum Thapsus L. Common Mullein.

This plant was not recognized by Chehalis, Lummi, and Swinomish informants, who were unanimous in the opinion that it is adventitious. It is; however, not listed by Jones as such for the Olympic Peninsula.

Scrophularia californica Cham. (*S. oregana* Pennell.) Figwort.

This plant was shown only to a Chehalis, who did not recognize it.

Mimulus guttatus DC. (*M. Langsdorfii* Donn.) Monkey Flower.

The Quinault called the monkey flower bam-asɪdixtcuspakan, "cool water grass," and the informant added that it grows along rivers; she calls it a buttercup in English. She knew no use for it. The Quileute informant did not know it at all.

Veronica americana Schwein. Speedwell.

This plant is known to the Quileute as xagai"ɪ'put, "frog leaves," since it grows in frog ponds. They do not use it. The Cowlitz informant did not know it.

Digitalis purpurea L. Foxglove.

This plant was discussed only with a Skokomish informant, who recognized it as an adventitious one, brought into the Skokomish valley by the first whites.

Castilleja angustifolia (Nutt.) Don. var. **Bradburii** Fern. Indian Paintbrush.

Makah	k'lik'lixuse'uk, "red top plant"
Quileute	pĭtcibixa'a, "red flowers"

Medicine. The Quileute make an infusion of the whole plant and drink it to bring about regularity in menstruation. It was carefully pointed out that this was very mild and not used as an abortive if there was any fear of pregnancy. After drinking this tea, the blood of a male fish duck was drunk.

Miscellaneous. The Quinault have no name for it, but know that it grows on the beach. The Klallam informant could not recall the name, but remembers eating the honey out of the blossoms as a child. The Makah have no use for it.[318] The Skokomish informant had seen it but did not have a name for it.

RUBIACEAE. Madder Family

Galium Aparine. Bedstraw.

Cowlitz	kamati'
Makah	qwiti'bupt
Snohomish	spē'b'kotsidats

Charms. The Cowlitz regard this plant as poisonous; and if a woman, using the right incantations, rubs herself with this while bathing, she will be successful in love; if, however, she fails to repeat the incantation correctly, she will get blotches on her face.

Miscellaneous. The Snohomish rub the body with a bundle of this plant after bathing. They evidently do not distinguish between this variety and the scented *G. triflorum*.

The Makah regard this as a sticky weed and do not use it.

Galium triflorum Michx. Scented Bedstraw.

Klallam	tīta'qwē'a'ĕltc
Lummi	qwai"ēsɛn
Makah	up'sɪ"ɪ
Quileute	kla'kaput
Skagit	tsibi'bkotsi

Medicine. The Lummi rub the body with this for a good smell, while the Quinault and Klallam mash it and put it on the hair. The Makah do the same, for it will make the hair grow. The Skagit do not use it.

Charms. A Quileute woman will get some hairs of the man she wishes to attract and press them with some of her own, together with some bedstraw. Just as they stick together so will this desired man stick to her. The woman who told the informant this had had eight husbands and as each died she did this and got another by the action.

Miscellaneous. It is doubtful whether there is much distinction made between the *Aparine* and *triflorum* varieties of bedstraw. The spread here may be due to the chance collection of specimens.

CAPRIFOLIACEAE. Honeysuckle Family

Sambucus callicarpa Greene. (*S. leiosperma* Leiberg.) Red Elderberry.

Chehalis	k'la'lxanł, whole bush; sk'la'lxan, berries
Cowlitz	t'cu'matas
Green River	sts'abta'ts, bush; sts'abt, berries[319]
Klallam	stsɪwukɪ'łtc, plant; stsɪ'wu'k^u, berries
Makah	tsɪkɪ''ĕ
Quileute	ts'pa''aput, whole plant; stsɪ'wu'k^u, berries
Quinault	k'lo'manix
Skagit	ts!a'bat
Skokomish	sk!a'lxad
Skykomish	ts'abtadts, whole plant; ts'abt, berries
Snohomish	s'tsa'bt
Squaxin	st'sa'btats, whole plant; st'sa'bt, berries
Swinomish	s'stap't

Food. The use of these berries is spread in the area far beyond even the list of people given here. The berries are always steamed on rocks and put in a container which is stored underground or in cool water. They are usually eaten in winter. In addition to the groups listed above, the berries are also eaten by the Lower Chinook.[320]

Medicine. The leaves are pounded fresh and put on an abscess or boil by the Makah.[321] The Cowlitz grind the leaves and put them on a sore joint to reduce the swelling. They also dip the bark in hot water and apply it to a swelling. The Squaxin mash the leaves and, after dipping the pulp in water, apply it to an area infected with blood poisoning. The Quinault scrape the bark and boil it. The liquid becomes milky, and this is put on a woman's breasts after childbirth to bring on a flow of milk.

Miscellaneous. The old Skykomish chiefs ordered the people not to fire brush where red elderberries grew, because the deer ate the ripe ones. The Swinomish informant named the plant, but said that it did not grow in their vicinity.

Literature. Reagan lists the following as the Quileute words for red elderberry and their derivation: tse-bah'put, tse-bah or che-lits-shalts-tse-wit tse-e-bah, chlits-shalts-tse-tut; "put," "tut," and "chlits" mean tree. He describes the method of preserving the berries and states that the bark and roots are used medicinally, being made into a tea used by women during confinement, and also for colds.[322] Stuhr states that a tea of the dry flowers of *S. canadensis* is used as a diaphoretic by the American Indians.[323]

Sambucus glauca Nutt. (*S. coerulea* Raf.) Blue Elderberry.

Chehalis	ts'ɑk'wik wunł, whole plant; ts'ɑk'wik'w, berry
Green River	tsikwɪ'q^w
Klallam	tseqwek^u
Lummi	tsɪkwɪ'k^u
Quinault	k'we'łap, bark of elderberry
Skagit	tsɪkwɪk^u
Skokomish	tsɪkwixɛd
Squaxin	t'sikwi'kwats, plant; t'sikwik^w, berries
Swinomish	tsɛqwɪ'uk

Food. The Klallam, Chehalis, Squaxin, and all others listed here prepared this elderberry in the same way as the red one. The Lower Chinook also use this berry, but do not find it in the profusion of the red elderberry.[324] The Lummi gather this berry by beating it from the bushes with a comb made of syringa. They go to the vicinity of Sumas to get it. The Skokomish informant remembers the berries as eaten fresh only.

Materials. The Quinault remove the pith from the stem and insert a plug, to make a whistle for calling elk.

Medicine. The Klallam steep the bark and drink the tea for diarrhoea. The Quinault use the same drink for an emetic.

Literature. The same information given by Reagan for the red elderberry is also true of the blue elderberry.

Linnaea borealis L., var. **longiflora** Torr. (*L. americana* of Piper Fl. Wash.; *L. borealis longiflora* of Piper Fl. Nw. Coast.) Twinflower.

This plant was discussed only with a Snohomish informant, who named it sto't'xodob and said the leaves are boiled to make a tea for colds.

Symphoricarpos albus (L.) Blake. (*S. racemosus* Michx.; *S. hyalinus* Heller.) Snowberry.

Chehalis	sk'awksi'nł
Green River	t'ɛda'xwdi[325]
Klallam	p'astciłxtc
Skagit	sɪ'sqwɪdats
Snohomish	kładiwa'dats
Squaxin	k'wala'stapats, whole plant; k'wla'stap, berries
Swinomish	sɪ'sqwɪdats, plant; skikai'yus, berry

Food. Although the Chehalis do not regard the berries as good and the children throw them at one another, the Squaxin, their neighbors, dry them. The Snohomish and Swinomish do not use the berries.

Medicine. The Chehalis rub the berries on the hair as soap. They also use the leaves by bruising and applying them to a cut as a poultice, or by

[319] Ballard.
[320] Miss Louise Colbert.
[321] Densmore, p. 316, lists the pounded root as a hair wash. A decoction of bark was also used to counteract an evil charm.
[322] Reagan, p. 69.
[323] Stuhr, No. 129.
[324] Miss Louise Colbert.
[325] Ballard.

washing the cut with an infusion made by boiling the leaves, or by chewing the leaves and spitting them on the injury. According to another informant, the Chehalis boil the bark of the roots and drink the tea three times a day as a cure for venereal diseases. The Green River people use the plant to disinfect a festering sore. The Skagit use the bark as a remedy for tuberculosis. A very mild tea of it is given a baby with a coated tongue. The berries are eaten as an antidote for poisoning. The Klallam boil the leaves for a cold cure.

Beliefs. The Green River tribe say that when these berries are plentiful, there will be many dog salmon, for this white berry is the eye of the dog salmon. The Cowlitz are not familiar with the plant.

Literature. Reagan states that the Quileute used the snowberries in ceremonies.[326] Stuhr lists the berries as a reputed emetic, agreeing with the Skagit.[327]

Lonicera ciliosa (Pursh) Poir. Orange Honeysuckle.

Chehalis	tsūma'nts, "it hugs a tree";
	k'ayukwunɬ, "swings on a tree"
Cowlitz	t'a'tcanminad'it
Klallam	snana'qwŭltc, "spook vine"
Lummi	k!ĭtě'ɫc
Skagit	yaidū"ats, "swing plant"
Snohomish	yaidō"ats
Squaxin	yaydu'wats
Swinomish	yaidū'wats, "swing plant" (yaidū', swing)

Medicine. The Swinomish boil the bark as a tea for colds and sore throat. More general in their use are the leaves, which the Swinomish bruise and soak in hot water. When this water is steaming, a woman holds her breasts over it to stimulate lacteal flow. The Swinomish also chew the leaves and swallow the juice for colds. The Chehalis have two very divergent uses for the leaves: (1) they are crushed in water used to bathe little girls to make their hair grow long and sleek; (2) the leaves are dipped in water which is drunk as a contraceptive. The Squaxin agree with this latter use and also drink this tea for "womb trouble." The Skagit boil the leaves and pour this juice over the plant which has been laid on the patient, as a strengthening tonic. The Lummi boil the leaves as a tea for tuberculosis. The Klallam chew the leaves to put on bruises.

Beliefs. The Snohomish, who do not use the plant, say the crows swing on it. The Cowlitz do not use it.

Lonicera involucrata (Richards.) Banks. Swamp Honeysuckle, Twinberry.

Green River	kakaɫě'xlits, "crow food"[328]
Makah	tcakat'kebupt, "crow plant"[329]

---

[326] Reagan, p. 68.
[327] Stuhr, p. 25.
[328] Ballard.
[329] Densmore, p. 318, lists an unidentified plant called chaa kabup from tcaa, "crow" and bup, "plant," meaning berries grown on purpose for the crows. From its description it would seem to be the same as *Lonicera involucrata.*

Quileute	ka'ayū'oput, "crow plant"
Quinault	kaxa'ltcilnix, "crow berries"
Skokomish	kakad'lĕx

Materials. The Quileute use the juice of the berries to paint the faces of dolls.

Medicine. Both the Quinault and the Makah women chew the leaves during confinement. The Quileute chew the leaves as an emetic when poisoned.

Miscellaneous. The Green River people do not use the plant, nor do the Skokomish.

It is remarkable that in every tribe listed the plant is associated with the crow.

CUCURBITACEAE. Gourd Family

Echinocystis oregana (T. & G.) Cogn. (*Micrampelis oregana* (T. & G.) Greene.) Old Man Root.

Chehalis	tsakatci'tlɑnt
Green River	q'sɛq'si, vine; dě'dibo', gourd[328]

Medicine. The Lower Chinook use the gourd as a poultice.[330] The Squaxin mash the upper stalk in water and dip aching hands into it. It is poisonous, as was proved by the son of a friend who ate some and died. The Chehalis burn the root, powder it; and mix it with bear grease to apply it to scrofula sores.

CAMPANULACEAE. Bellflower Family

Campanula rotundifolia L. Bluebell.

This flower was shown only to a Squaxin informant, who did not recognize it.

COMPOSITAE. Composite Family

Solidago vespertina Piper. (*S. Purshii* of Piper Fl. Wash.) Goldenrod.

This plant was discussed with Chehalis and Squaxin informants, neither of whom knew it. The Chehalis informant said it was introduced and a bad weed.

Adenocaulon bicolor Hook. Silvergreen.

Only the Cowlitz, of the three informants shown this plant, had a name for it. She called it tsati'mas and said the leaves were bruised and applied to a boil to draw it out. The Chehalis did not know it and the Squaxin, although she had no name for it, knew that the leaves were crushed and used as a poultice on scrofula sores.

Anaphalis margaritacea (L.) Benth. & Hook., var. **subalpina** Gray. Pearly Everlasting.

Makah	kla"stupbupt
Quileute	sīsība'xɬwa (same name for yarrow)

Medicine. The Quileute use the whole plant for a steam bath to cure rheumatism. *Stachys ciliata* is used for the same purpose.

---

[330] Miss Louise Colbert.

Beliefs. The Makah do not allow children to play with this plant, because it makes sores. The Quinault had no name and no use for it.

Literature. Stuhr refers to its aromatic quality, which is probably what dictates the Quileute use.[331]

Eriophyllum lanatum (Pursh) Forbes. (*Bahia lanata* Nutt.) Woolly Sunflower.

Medicine. Only the Chehalis informant knew a native name for this plant. She called it k'we'xkwixk'alaxkum, derived from k'wek, yellow, and yalakum, prairie. The dried flower is mixed with grease and a person of the opposite sex is touched with it as a love charm. The informant related that her uncle was "doped" with it by an old woman and nearly drowned getting to her. The Skagit informant knew no name for the plant but said the leaves were rubbed on the face to prevent chapping.

Miscellaneous. The Squaxin informant did not know it, and the Lummi recognized it as a plant that grew beyond Marietta.

Achillea Millefolium L. Yarrow.

Chehalis	kwayu·'hayipsnł, "squirrel tail"
Cowlitz	wəpənwə'pən
Klallam	s'qwuntayiłtc
Lummi	telai"uqwa'pł
Makah	k!astub'bupt
Quileute	sīsiba'xłwuput, "for smelling leaves"
Quinault	ləko'stap
Skagit	sī'colts
Snohomish	kĕkedŏ'xub, "little squirrel tail" (probably chipmunk)
Squaxin	sqikdzu'xap, "squirrel tail" (sqadza, "squirrel"; dzu'xap, "tail")
Swinomish	ci'ciltsats

Medicine. The medicinal quality of this plant was as well known to the Indians of this region as to the old herb dealers. Its aromatic properties were recognized by the Swinomish in its use as a bath for invalids, and the Quileute boiled the leaves in the room where an infant was sick to make it smell pleasantly. The Cowlitz soak the leaves for a hair wash.

For a stronger use Makah women eat the leaves raw to produce sweating at childbirth, boil them and drink the tea to purify the blood, and drink a stronger solution to heal the uterus after birth. The Klallam use a similar tea during childbirth and for colds as well, mixing it for the latter with wild cherry bark. The Quinault boil the roots for tuberculosis and also use the tea as an eye wash. The Cowlitz and Squaxin believe the same tea is effective for stomach trouble. The Chehalis boil the leaves and drink the tea to stop the passage of blood with diarrhoea. Before the coming of the whites they were subject to this illness

from eating too much raw meat, according to one informant. The Skagit and Snohomish also use this diarrhoea remedy.

The plant is used as a general tonic by the Quinault by boiling the roots. The Lummi boil the flowers and drink the tea to relieve body aches, and one informant feels she did not get mumps from her children because of this use. This drink produces sweating, as does the Makah preparation used at childbirth.

Yarrow is also used as a poultice, the Klallam chewing the leaves and putting them on sores. The Squaxin smash the flower to use the same way. The Quileute lay the boiled leaves on rheumatic limbs and reduce fever with them.

Literature. Stuhr lists yarrow as an aromatic herb and states that the American Indians use the leaves as tea and poultice for skin rash.[332]

Chrysanthemum Leucanthemum L. Ox-eye Daisy.

Quileute	k'eba' xpixłila, "little white flowers"
Snohomish	tsikai'tsub (generic name for any flower)

Medicine. Only the Quileute use it. They dry the flowers and stems, boil them, and use the wash for chapped hands.

Miscellaneous. There was considerable discussion with informants as to whether this plant was indigenous. The Squaxin informant did not know it; the Quinault said it was a new growth brought by the whites, to which the Skagit agreed. The Lummi felt it had always been here but did not know it, and the Snohomish said there may always have been a few but they have become plentiful in recent years.

Petasites speciosus (Nutt.) Piper. Common Coltsfoot.

Lummi	suk'tcen
Quileute	qwai"ĕxput
Quinault	qwai"ax
Skagit	yĕcĕ'yuqwats

Food. The Quinault say the Muckleshoot eat the stems boiled but the Quinault do not. Its use as food was found nowhere else.

Material. The Quinault use the leaves to cover berries when cooking them in a pit.

Medicine. The root is used as cough medicine by the Quileute either boiled to make a tea or eaten raw. The Quinault smash the root and soak it as a wash for swellings and sore eyes. The Skagit warm the leaves and lay them on parts afflicted with rheumatism. They also boil the root to make a drink for tuberculosis patients when they spit blood, while the Lummi use the same drink as an emetic.

Cirsium sp. Thistle.

Medicine. Only the Lummi use the thistle and they boil the roots and tips in salt water to drink at childbirth.[333]

[331] Stuhr, p. 29.
[332] *Ibid.,* p. 28.
[333] Stern, p. 14.

Arctium minus (Hill) Bernh. Burdock.

| Cowlitz | tcuktcu'k |
| Skagit | xĕxĕ'bats, "sticks to everything" |

Medicine. The Cowlitz boil the roots and drink the infusion for whooping cough.

Miscellaneous. The Swinomish know it only as the "bad plant." The Skagit say it came with the whites in hayseed. The Lummi say the Chinese and Japanese eat the roots, and the burrs stick to horses and wool. They have no name for it. The Snohomish say the plant is introduced. Jones agrees with this.

MISCELLANEOUS PLANTS

Gathered into this group are the scattered examples of fungi, algae, lichens, and mosses, many of them not well identified.

FUNGI

Fomes sp. Bracket Fungus.

Cowlitz	tialaxo'xo
Quinault	t'owole
Snohomish	p'lólqwat

Medicine. Only the Makah make real use of this fungus. They scrape it on a sharp rock and use the powder as a body deodorant.

Miscellaneous. The Quinault have the belief that since this fungus is ear-shaped it sends sounds back and causes echoes.[334] Both the Chehalis and Snohomish use the fungus as a target for archery. The Cowlitz draw pictures on it, and the Quileute note its position on a tree as a guide in returning home from hunting trips.

ALGAE

Ulva lactuca. Sea Lettuce.

The Quileute call this kłop'tsai'yup, "green ocean leaves," and apply it to sunburned lips because of its cooling qualities. The Quinault informant did not know it.

Crab Seaweed

The Makah call this xala'wick!bupt. It is laid on the breasts of a new mother to stimulate lacteal flow.

Tall Seaweed

The Makah eat the holdfasts of this seaweed, which they call kałkatsup.

---

[334] Olson, p. 165; substantiated by present informant as well.

Fucus sp. Rockweed or Bladderwrack.

| Makah | kaka'lak!oka dub |
| Quileute | xopiki'sta, "little kelps" or "babies of big kelps" |

The Makah children let dried pieces of this seaweed race on the beach in the wind. The Quileute do not use it.

Miscellaneous Seaweeds

All seaweed is called kaxı'ati'xłkło'ob by the Quileute. They gather seaweed and burn it when a strong wind is blowing, believing that the wind, when it smells the acrid odor, will go away. Women whose husbands are at sea do this. The Makah use seaweed to chink the cracks in their houses.

Nereocystis luetkeana. Kelp.

| Quileute | xopı''ıkis |
| Quinault | k'otk'a' |

Kelp is very useful in a fishing culture for fish line. The Quileute, Quinault, and Makah all use the long end for that purpose. The Quinault use this line especially for halibut, sole, and cod. The bottle end is used by all these same tribes for carrying fish oil and, later, molasses.

The Makah children make little wagons with wheels cut of rounds of kelp and also drag the stems along the beach and play at harpooning whales.

Literature. Reagan states that some tribes eat the dried kelp, flaked like chipped beef.[335]

LICHEN

Foliaceous Lichen

Only one lichen was discussed and that with the Quinault, who call it ts'o'o'tc. It grows on trees and is used to wipe salmon when it is cleaned. Fish should not be washed because that toughens the skin.

MOSSES

Sphagnum sp. Sphagnum.

| Makah | pū'ā'p |
| Quinault | tsŏ'ŏtciłminix, "berry moss" |

The Makah use sphagnum to dress wounds, a use found for it during the first World War. Its absorptive qualities are recognized by Chinook women who use it for sanitary napkins. It is also widely used as camp bedding.

---

[335] Reagan, p. 70.

APPENDIX I:

ADDITIONS TO THE QUILEUTE ENTRIES
BY J. V. POWELL AND FRED WOODRUFF[1]

Sword Fern (p. 13)

pilápila, general term for all ferns; pilápilapat, fern plants;[2] ts'ikʷí, fern roots (the "name" ts'át t'óts'a means "new growth" and can be applied to any growing thing)

Lady Fern (p. 14)

ts'ikʷí, fern roots (general for all ferns)

Maidenhair Fern (p. 14)

pilápila, fern (the form quoted from Reagan includes the demonstrative)

Brake Fern (p. 14)

q'aqʷa?ápat

Deer Fern (p. 15)

lakʷa?á•, to wipe (the name lakʷacicí•qʷoł is not recalled by the informant)

Common Scouring-rush (p. 15)

silatc'íłpat, "plant that makes a rasping noise"

Giant Horsetail (p. 15)

t'ot'ó•tsi; ts'í•xak, bulblike roots of giant horsetail

Western Yew (p. 16)

xi•yá

Sitka Spruce (p. 17)

yáksa

Hemlock (p. 17)

tí•ła

Douglas Fir (p. 19)

tł'íxits

Western Red Cedar (p. 19)

ts'a•pis; ts'apístc'it, thick, outside bark; sikʷ'o•ya, soft, inside bark

Cat-tail (p. 21)

síts'ay

Surf-grass (p. 21)

xá•k', "it's hard"

Rye-grass (p. 21)

k'ák'ipat, "strong plant"; the braided root bundles used for rubbing the body are x̣ʷats'á•til

Skunk Cabbage (p. 22)

t'ó•qʷ'a; t'o•qʷ'a?aq'i•ts'a, seeds or berries of skunk cabbage; t'o•qʷ'ats'a?boqʷł, skunk cabbage roots

Camas (p. 24)

kʷá•la

Tiger Lily (p. 25)

(?); the common water lily is pispilákstc'iyił, "liver-shaped leaves"

Twisted-stalk (p. 25)

yáe?iwapat, "snake plant"

Wild Lily-of-the-valley (p. 25)

ts'i?ats'íłpat, "sour plant"

Trillium (p. 25)

kʷ'okʷ'òtstadaktc'iyíł, "thieves' leaves"

Cottonwood (p. 26)

kʷ:o?doqʷ'

Willow (p. 26)

łilá•q'a

Nettle (p. 28)

padá•kʷoqʷoł

Spring Beauty, Miner's Lettuce (p. 29)

p'ip'itc'its'í•p, "red things next to the ground"

Anemone (p. 29)

t'a?o•l is a sea anemone; no word is known for a plant by that name. See also Buttercup, p. 29

Columbine (p. 30)

p'itc'abixa?a'•, "red flowers"; the informant feels that this is not a name, but a comment

Saxifrage (p. 31)

wawoxʷtc'iyíła, "having fuzzy hairs on its leaves"; qʷa?latc'iyíła, "three leaves"

Skunk Currant, Wild Currant (p. 32)

tł'ilo•?o

Goats' Beard (p. 33)

tł'ilí•lix

Wild Rose (p. 34)

tł'iqʷ'ay

Thimbleberry (p. 34)

t'aq'á•tcił

Salmonberry (p. 35)

tc'a?áłwa; yatctc'ił?at, salmonberry shoots; tc'á?ałwa tł'o?ó•tc'ył, salmonberry leaves

Blackberry, Dewberry (p. 35)

badá?abixʷ; the name cicipq'í•ts'a, "black berries," is now often used

Wild Strawberry (p. 36)

t'obí•ya, "pick them up"

Silverweed (p. 37)

tł'itł'í•cit; also, ła?it'aẏ, "gathering hands"

Yellow Avens (p. 37)

kʷoloqʷoł, probably the same as baneberry, p. 30; hat'alitc'iyíł, hair seal leaves

[1] From "A Note on the Quileute Entries of *Ethnobotany of Western Washington*" by J. V. Powell and Fred Woodruff, in *Studies in Northwest Indian Languages,* edited by James E. Hoard and Thomas H. Hess (Sacramento Anthropological Society Paper, 11, April 1971).

[2] The Quileute lexical suffix "-yat," meaning "tree, bush, plant," could be attached to nearly all of the plants, berries, fruit, or trees listed herein. For that reason, we are not listing such forms unless the plant is generally referred to with the suffixial form.

Crab Apple (p. 38)
siyoyóxk'idax, "hurts the tongue"
Giant Vetch (p. 39)
babidaqᵂółpat, "string bean plant"
Wood-sorrel (p. 39)
(?) These names are no longer remembered
Broadleaf Maple (p. 39)
la?á•xał
Vine Maple (p. 40)
t'apsiyóqᵂpat, roots; laláqᵂts'ił
Cascara (p. 40)
?akílipat, "bear plant"
Cow Parsnip (p. 42)
tł'ó•pit; the basket woven of cow parsnip stems is
tł'o•pitbay
Fool's Huckleberry (p. 44)
ticoqᵂ'ótłipat, "bottom grass plant"
Salal (p. 43)
kᵂo?ó•d
Red Huckleberry (p. 44)
tiło?ot
Fern Mint (p. 45)
tł'otł'opabíxa?a•, "they are blue flowers"; possible
this is not a name but a comment
Hedge Nettle, Woundwort (p. 45)
sisí•bał
Indian Paintbrush (p. 46)
p'itc'ibíxa?a•
Bedstraw (p. 46)
tł'apá?pat, "bed plant"
Red Elderberry (p. 47)
ts'ibá•; ts'iwókᵂ is a loanword into Quileute
Swamp Honeysuckle, Twinberry (p. 48)
ká?ayo?pat, "crow plant"

Pearly Everlasting and Yarrow (pp. 48-49)
sisi?báłwa
Ox-eye Daisy (p. 49)
q'abałbíxa?a•, "white flower"
Common Coltsfoot (p. 49)
qᵂ'ayíxpat
Rockweed, Bladderwrack (p. 50)
xᵂopik'ísis'a, "little kelp"
Kelp (p. 50)
xᵂopík'is
Moss (p. 50)
qᵂ'ayocí, underwater moss; t'owá•?as, tree moss

It may be a matter of interest to include those
botanical terms extant for the other Chimakuan
language, Chimakum (Chemacum). These forms
have been taken from notes by Franz Boas, made
available to the author by the Library of the American Philosophical Society.

Blackberry (p. 35)
to•?otxᵂoqᵂ'a; q'i•ts'a, berry (general)
Cedar bark (p. 19)
so•kᵂ'om
Grass
tł'o•?ob; łapitsa
Nettle (p. 28)
tł'alap, tł'alilap (pl.)
Pine (p. 16)
qaxᵂotc'a
Raspberry
xatc'it'ida?a (prob. hatc'it'ida?a), "good tasting"
Salmonberry (p. 35)
?ali•lo•; tsiyi•lapat, salmonberry bush

APPENDIX II: PLANTS DISCUSSED IN THE TEXT

LIST OF PLANTS	CHEHALIS	COWLITZ	GREEN RIVER	KLALLAM	L. CHINOOK	LUMMI	MAKAH	NISQUALLY	PUYALLUP	QUILEUTE	QUINAULT	SAMISH	SKAGIT	SKOKOMISH	SNOHOMISH	SNUQUALMIE	SQUAXIN	SWINOMISH
Licorice Fern		X	X	X		X	X				X		X		X			X
Sword Fern	X	X	X	X		X	X			X	X		X		X		X	X
Wood Fern		X	X	X											X			
Lady Fern		X		X			X			X	X							
Maidenhair Fern			X			X	X			X	X			X				
Brake Fern	X	X	X	X	X	X	X			X	X		X	X	X		X	X
Deer Fern							X			X	X							
Scouring Rush		X								X	X		X					
Horsetail		X		X	X		X				X		X					X
Field Horsetail					X													
Yew	X	X		X			X				X	X	X		X			X
White Pine						X					X		X					
Lodgepole Pine											X							
Spruce							X			X	X							X
Hemlock	X	X		X		X	X			X	X		X		X			X
Fir	X	X	X	X		X	X		X	X	X		X		X	X	X	X
Cedar	X	X		X		X	X	X		X	X		X	X	X	X	X	X
Juniper																		
Cat-tail	X	X		X	X		X				X				X		X	
Surf-grass							X			X	X							
Rye-grass							X				X							
Sedge							X											
Cotton Sedge							X											
Tule				X			X				X		X					
Skunk Cabbage		X		X	X		X			X	X	X		X				X
Rush (Juncus effusus)											X					X		
Rush (J. xiphioides)							X			X	X	X						X
Bear grass	X	X		X							X							
Death Camas	X																X	
Hellebore		X									X							
Wild Onion				X			X				X						X	
Brodiaea																	X	
Camas	X	X		X	X	X	X	X	X	X	X		X				X	
Fawn Lily											X							X
Tiger Lily				X		X	X			X	X		X	X	X			X
Clintonia		X																
Twisted-stalk							X				X							
Fairy Bells						X	X	X					X					X
Lily-of-the-Valley						X	X	X		X	X		X		X			
Trillium							X	X		X	X		X		X			X
Rattlesnake Plantain		X		X							X						X	
Cottonwood	X	X	X	X							X							
Willow	X	X		X		X	X			X	X		X		X		X	
Hazelnut	X	X				X	X			X	X		X	X	X		X	X
Alder		X		X	X	X	X			X	X						X	
Oak	X	X		X				X			X						X	
Nettle	X	X		X		X	X				X	X	X	X	X		X	X
Wild Ginger			X			X					X						X	
Sheep-sorrel Dock	X																X	
Bitter Dock											X							
Dock sp.	X	X																
Sand Verbena				X			X											
Spring Beauty		X				X				X	X		X		X			
Water Lily							X				X							
Anemone		X								X								
Buttercup							X				X			X	X			
Larkspur	X		X							X							X	
Columbine	X	X	X							X			X				X	
Baneberry										X	X				X			

LIST OF PLANTS	CHEHALIS	COWLITZ	GREEN RIVER	KLALLAM	L. CHINOOK	LUMMI	MAKAH	NISQUALLY	PUYALLUP	QUILEUTE	QUINAULT	SAMISH	SKAGIT	SKOKOMISH	SNOHOMISH	SNUQUALMIE	SQUAXIN	SWINOMISH
Oregon Grape	X	X		X	X	X	X				X	X	X		X		X	X
Vanilla Leaf		X					X					X	X		X			
Bleeding-heart		X	X								X	X	X					
Stonecrop							X				X	X						
Boykinia										X	X							
Tiarella											X	X						
Fringe-cup												X						
Alumroot												X						
Youth-on-age		X					X											
Mock-orange		X			X								X		X			
Gooseberry		X		X		X	X	X				X	X		X			X
Swamp Currant						X							X		X			X
Skunk Currant			X				X			X			X					X
Trailing Currant			X			X	X					X	X	X				X
Red-flowering Currant				X														
Ninebark	X		X														X	
Ocean Spray	X			X		X	X						X		X		X	X
Spirea	X							X			X						X	
Hardhack			X			X								X	X			
Goat's-beard				X		X	X			X		X						
Rosa pisocarpa	X												X		X		X	
Rose sp.	X	X		X		X				X	X	X	X		X		X	X
Thimbleberry	X	X		X		X	X			X	X		X	X	X		X	X
Salmonberry	X	X	X	X	X	X	X				X	X					X	X
Blackcap		X	X	X				X	X									
Wild Blackberry		X	X			X		X	X	X		X			X			
Evergreen Blackberry		X																
Blackberry sp.				X	X						X							
Strawberry	X	X		X	X		X	X	X	X	X		X				X	X
Potentilla	X				X		X			X	X						X	X
Yellow Avens	X	X		X						X	X	X					X	
Wild Cherry			X			X					X		X	X	X			X
Squaw Plum	X	X				X					X		X	X	X		X	X
Serviceberry	X			X	X	X							X	X	X			X
Crab Apple		X	X	X	X		X			X	X	X						X
Lupine	X	X			X												X	
Clover							X											
Giant Vetch							X			X	X							
Vetch	X											X		X			X	
Lotus	X																	
Geranium	X	X															X	
Wood-sorrel		X					X			X								
Maple	X	X		X		X	X				X	X	X	X	X		X	X
Vine Maple	X	X		X		X				X	X		X	X	X		X	X
Cascara	X	X	X	X		X	X			X	X		X		X		X	X
Yellow Violet				X		X												
Cactus						X												
Soapberry						X												
Fireweed		X		X			X			X	X		X	X				X
Devil's Club		X	X	X		X							X			X		X
Sanicle	X																	
Sweet Cicely						X							X					X
Cow Parsnip					X		X			X	X							
Poison Hemlock			X												X			
Wild Celery		X			X		X			X				X		X		
Dogwood			X	X		X					X		X		X	X		X
Bunchberry						X					X							
Labrador Tea			X			X					X							
Rhododendron															X			
False Huckleberry										X	X							
Salal				X	X		X			X	X	X	X	X	X			X

LIST OF PLANTS	CHEHALIS	COWLITZ	GREEN RIVER	KLALLAM	L. CHINOOK	LUMMI	MAKAH	NISQUALLY	PUYALLUP	QUILEUTE	QUINAULT	SAMISH	SKAGIT	SKOKOMISH	SNOHOMISH	SNUQUALMIE	SQUAXIN	SWINOMISH
Madrona	X			X	X		X			X	X			X			X	
Kinnikinnick	X			X	X		X			X	X			X			X	
Evergreen Huckleberry					X						X							
Blue Huckleberry				X	X		X			X	X							
Red Huckleberry				X	X	X	X			X	X		X	X	X			X
Cranberry				X	X		X				X							
Star Flower		X									X							
Ash		X																
Waterleaf		X																
Mint	X	X																
Self Heal	X			X			X			X	X		X		X			X
Hedge Nettle			X			X	X		X	X	X		X					
Horehound		X																
Mullein	X					X												X
Figwort	X																	
Monkey Flower										X	X							
Speedwell		X									X							
Indian Paintbrush				X			X			X	X		X					
Bedstraw		X			X	X	X			X	X		X	X	X			
Red Elderberry	X	X	X	X	X	X	X			X	X		X	X	X		X	X
Blue Elderberry	X		X	X	X	X					X		X	X			X	X
Twinflower															X			
Snowberry	X	X	X	X									X		X		X	X
Honeysuckle	X	X		X		X							X		X		X	X
Twinberry	X		X		X		X			X	X		X					
Old Man Root	X		X		X												X	
Silvergreen	X	X															X	
Pearly Everlasting							X			X	X						X	
Goldenrod	X																X	
Woolly Sunflower	X					X							X				X	X
Yarrow	X	X		X		X	X			X	X		X		X		X	X
Ox-eye Daisy	X					X				X	X		X		X		X	
Coltsfoot						X				X	X		X					
Thistle						X												
Burdock		X				X							X		X			X

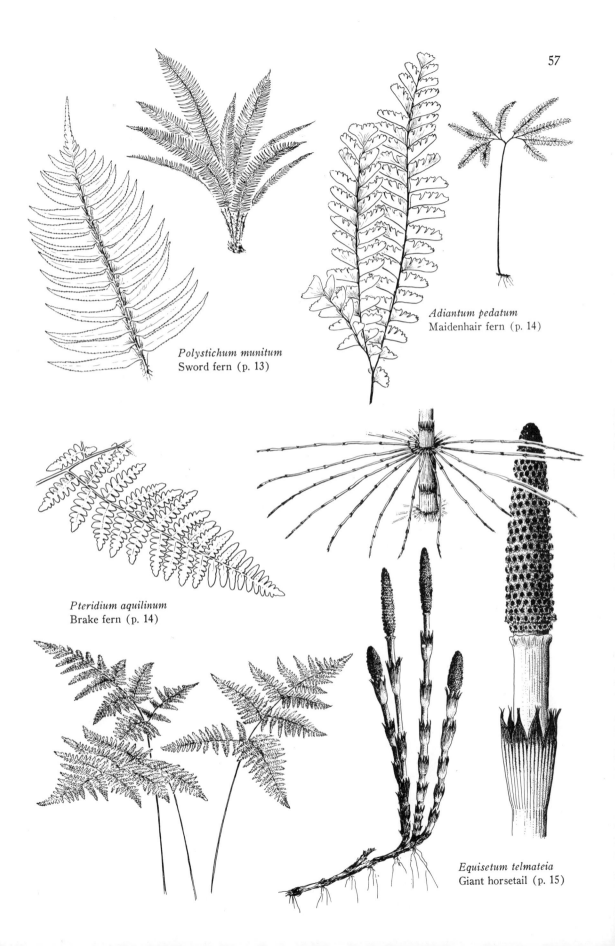

Polystichum munitum
Sword fern (p. 13)

Adiantum pedatum
Maidenhair fern (p. 14)

Pteridium aquilinum
Brake fern (p. 14)

Equisetum telmateia
Giant horsetail (p. 15)

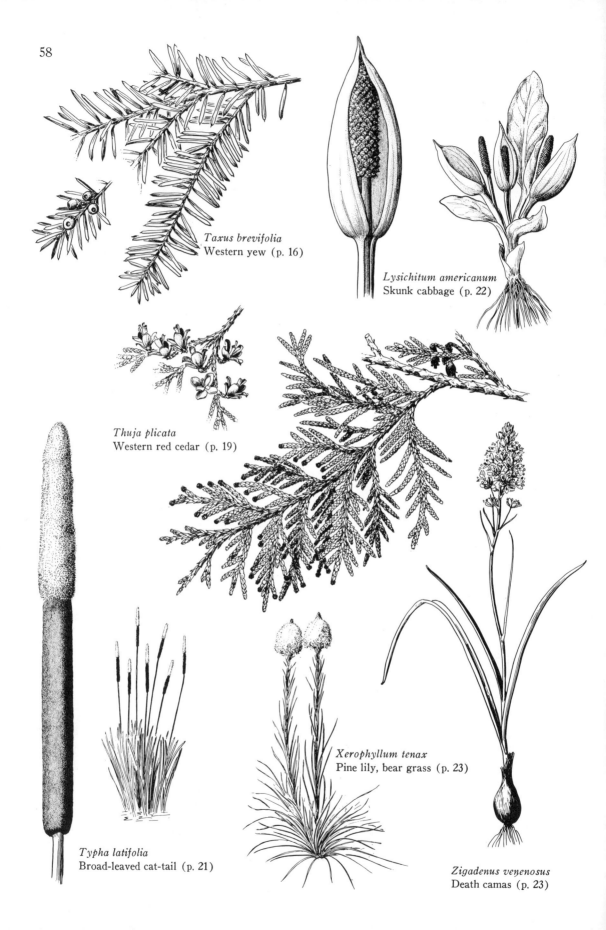

58

Taxus brevifolia
Western yew (p. 16)

Lysichitum americanum
Skunk cabbage (p. 22)

Thuja plicata
Western red cedar (p. 19)

Typha latifolia
Broad-leaved cat-tail (p. 21)

Xerophyllum tenax
Pine lily, bear grass (p. 23)

Zigadenus veṇenosus
Death camas (p. 23)

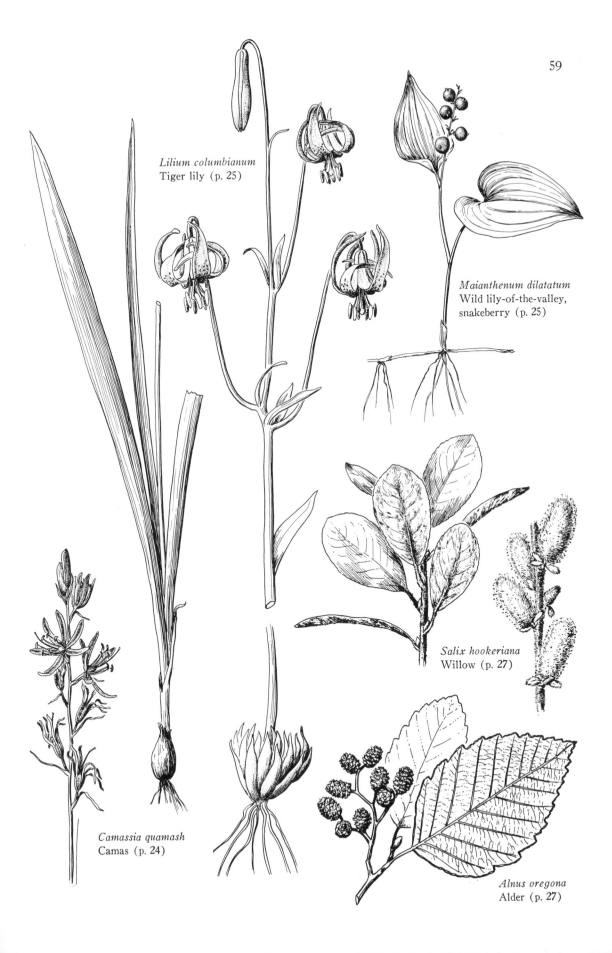

Lilium columbianum
Tiger lily (p. 25)

Maianthenum dilatatum
Wild lily-of-the-valley,
snakeberry (p. 25)

Salix hookeriana
Willow (p. 27)

Camassia quamash
Camas (p. 24)

Alnus oregona
Alder (p. 27)

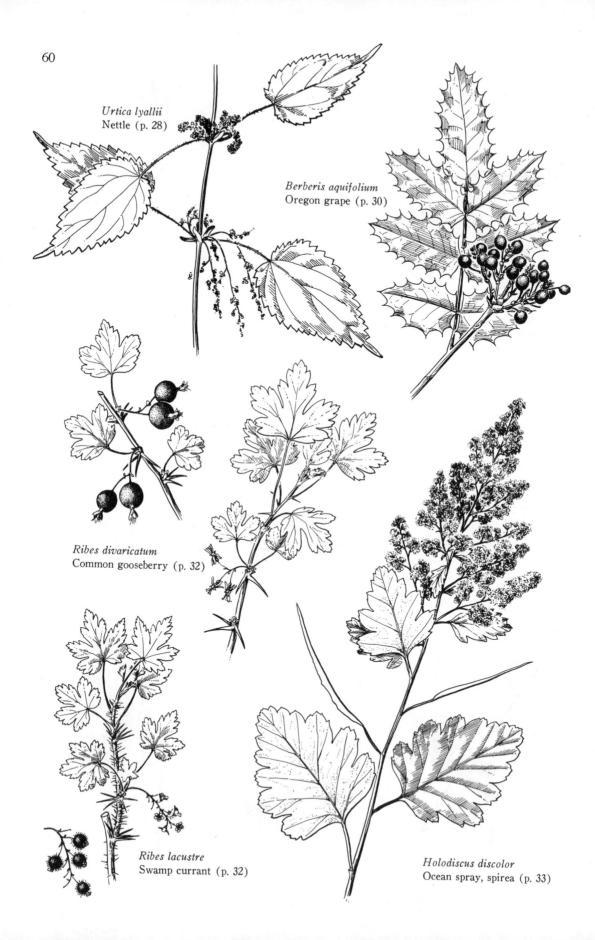

Urtica lyallii
Nettle (p. 28)

Berberis aquifolium
Oregon grape (p. 30)

Ribes divaricatum
Common gooseberry (p. 32)

Ribes lacustre
Swamp currant (p. 32)

Holodiscus discolor
Ocean spray, spirea (p. 33)

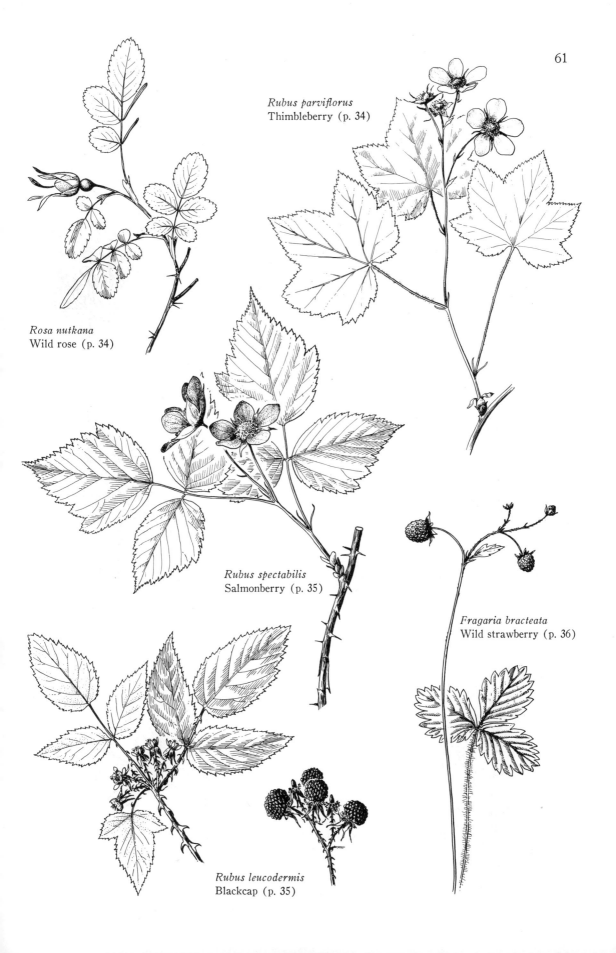

61

Rubus parviflorus
Thimbleberry (p. 34)

Rosa nutkana
Wild rose (p. 34)

Rubus spectabilis
Salmonberry (p. 35)

Fragaria bracteata
Wild strawberry (p. 36)

Rubus leucodermis
Blackcap (p. 35)

Acer macrophyllum
Broadleaf maple, Oregon maple (p. 39)

Prunus emarginata
Wild cherry (p. 37)

Osmaronia cerasiformis
Oso berry, squaw plum, Indian plum (p. 37)

Pyrus diversifolia
Crab apple (p. 38)

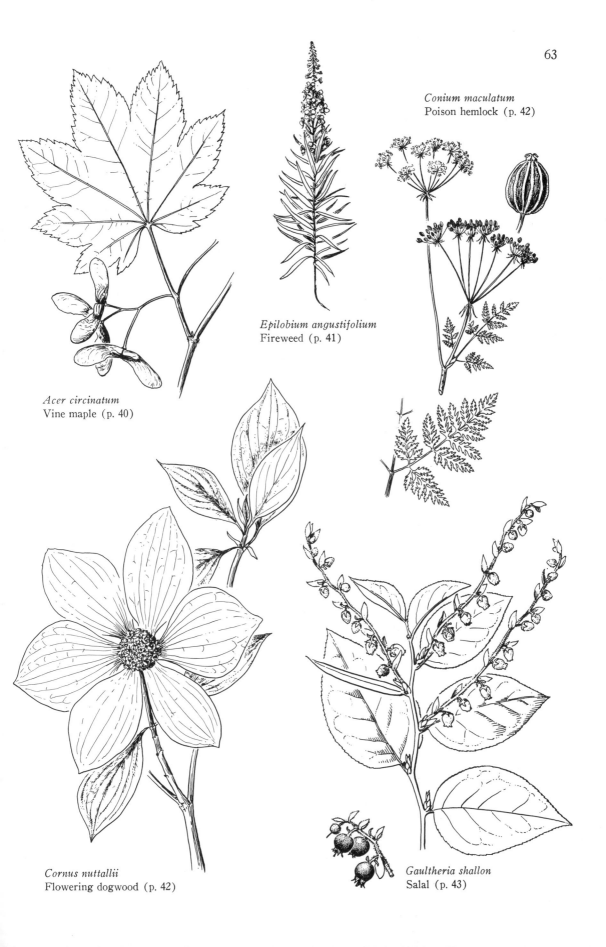

Conium maculatum
Poison hemlock (p. 42)

Epilobium angustifolium
Fireweed (p. 41)

Acer circinatum
Vine maple (p. 40)

Cornus nuttallii
Flowering dogwood (p. 42)

Gaultheria shallon
Salal (p. 43)

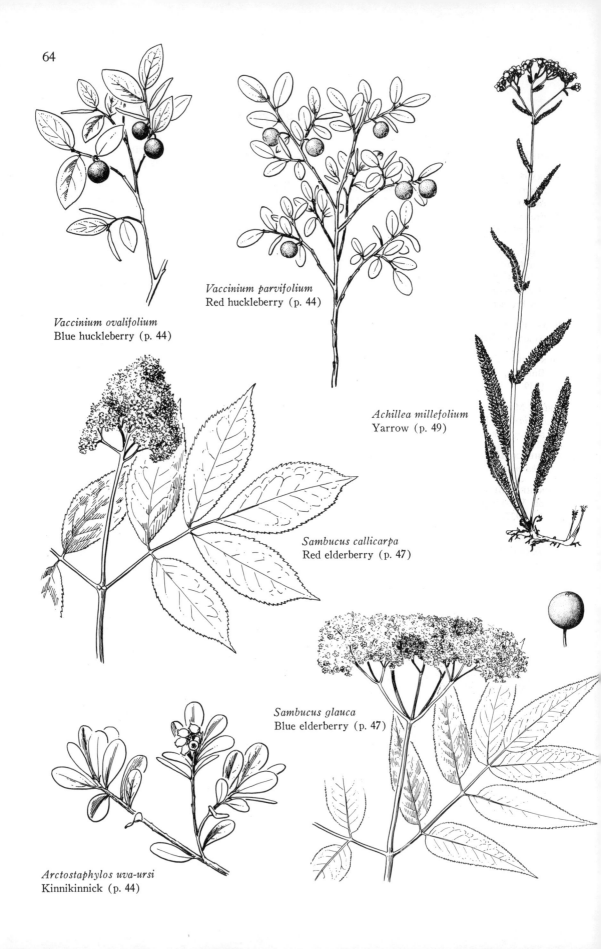

Vaccinium parvifolium
Red huckleberry (p. 44)

Vaccinium ovalifolium
Blue huckleberry (p. 44)

Achillea millefolium
Yarrow (p. 49)

Sambucus callicarpa
Red elderberry (p. 47)

Sambucus glauca
Blue elderberry (p. 47)

Arctostaphylos uva-ursi
Kinnikinnick (p. 44)

BIBLIOGRAPHY

ADAMSON, THELMA. Manuscript Notes on Chehalis.

ANDRADE, MANUEL J. "Quileute." (In *Handbook of American Indian Languages*, Bulletin, Bureau of American Ethnology, 40, pt. 3, 1933-1938, ed. by Franz Boas.) *Quileute Texts*, Columbia University Contributions to Anthropology, 12, 1931.

BALLARD, ARTHUR C. *Some Tales of the Southern Puget Sound Salish*, University of Washington Publications in Anthropology, 2, 1927. *Mythology of Southern Puget Sound*, University of Washington Publications in Anthropology, 3, 1929.

BOAS, FRANZ. *Chinook Texts*, Bulletin, Bureau of American Ethnology, 20, 1894.

DENSMORE, FRANCES. *Nootka and Quileute Music*, Bulletin, Bureau of American Ethnology, 124, 1939.

EELLS, MYRON. *The Twana, Chemakum and Klallam Indians of Washington Territory*, Report, Smithsonian Institution, 1886-1887, pp. 605-681.

GATHERCOAL, EDMUND N. AND WIRTH, ELMER H. *Pharmacognosy*, Philadelphia, 1936.

GUNTHER, ERNA. *Klallam Ethnography*, University of Washington Publications in Anthropology, 1, 1927.

HAEBERLIN, HERMANN AND GUNTHER, ERNA. *The Indians of Puget Sound*, University of Washington Publications in Anthropology, 4, 1930.

HASKINS, LESLIE. *Wild Flowers of the Pacific Coast*, Portland, 1934.

HITCHCOCK, C. LEO, ARTHUR CRONQUIST, MARION OWNBEY, AND J. W. THOMPSON, *Vascular Plants of the Pacific Northwest*, University of Washington Publications in Biology, 17, 5 vols. University of Washington Press, Seattle, 1955-1969.

JONES, GEORGE NEVILLE. *A Botanical Survey of the Olympic Peninsula*, University of Washington Publications in Biology, 5, 1936.

MUENSCHER, WALTER CONRAD LEOPOLD. *Poisonous Plants of the United States*, New York, 1939.

NEWCOMBE, C. F. (Editor) *Menzies' Journal of Vancouver's Voyage*, Archives of British Columbia, Memoir no. 5, Victoria, B. C., 1923.

OLSON, RONALD L. *The Quinault Indians*, University of Washington Publications in Anthropology, 6, 1936.

RAY, VERNE F. *Lower Chinook Ethnographic Notes*, University of Washington Publications in Anthropology, 7, 1938.

REAGAN, ALBERT. *Plants Used by the Hoh and Quileute Indians*, Transactions of the Kansas Academy of Science, 37, 1934.

SMITH, MARIAN W. *Puyallup-Nisqually*, Columbia University Contributions to Anthropology, 32, 1940.

STERN, BERNHARD. *The Lummi Indians of Northwest Washington*, Columbia University Contributions to Anthropology, 17, 1934.

STUHR, ERNST T. *Manual of Pacific Coast Drug Plants*, 1933.

SWAN, JAMES G. *The Indians of Cape Flattery*, Smithsonian Contributions to Knowledge, no. 220, Washington, 1869.

SWAN, JAMES G. *The Northwest Coast; or Three Years' Residence in Washington Territory*, New York, 1857; Washington Paperback edition, University of Washington Press, Seattle, 1972.

THWAITES, REUBEN GOLD (Editor). *Original Journals of the Lewis and Clark Expedition, 1804-1806 (etc.)*, New York, 1904-1905, 8 vols.

YOUNGKEN, HEBER W. *A Textbook of Pharmacognosy*, Philadelphia, 1936.

INDEX

*Indian informant.

*Indian informant.

*Indian informant.

*Indian informant.

*Indian informant.